NOOKS AND CORNERS OF PEMBROKESHIRE.

The Rood Screen
St Davids Cathedral

H.T. Timmins

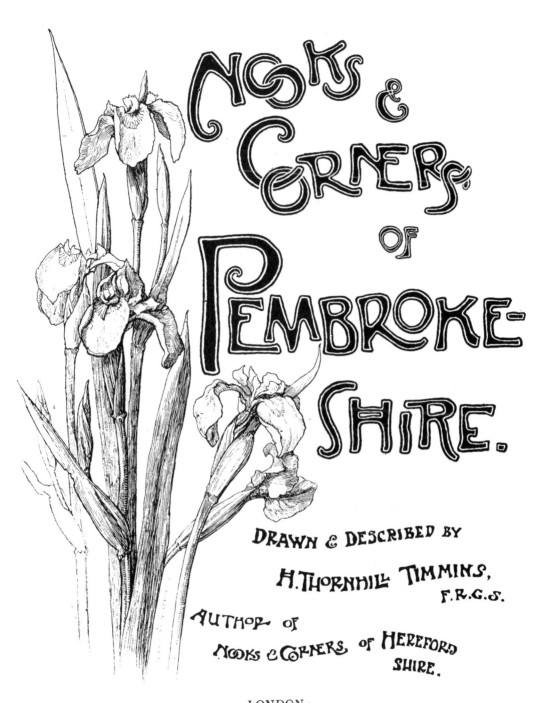

Nooks & Corners of Pembroke-Shire.

DRAWN & DESCRIBED BY

H. Thornhill Timmins,
F.R.G.S.

AUTHOR OF
NOOKS & CORNERS OF HEREFORD
SHIRE.

LONDON:
ELLIOT STOCK, 62, PATERNOSTER ROW, E.C.
1895.

Nooks and Corners of Pembrokeshire
was first published in 1895
by Elliot Stock, London

Reprinted by Lapridge Publications 1997

ISBN 1 899290 06 0

LAPRIDGE PUBLICATIONS
25 Church Street
Hereford HR1 2LR
Telephone 01432 353586

Printed and bound by
Redwood Books
Trowbridge

INTRODUCTION TO THIS NEW EDITION

The first edition, indeed, the only edition until now, of Henry Thornhill Timmins's *Nooks and Corners of Pembrokeshire* first appeared in 1895, just over a hundred years ago. Copies of that 1895 edition are difficult to find now and expensive. Bound in decorated cloth with bevelled boards and title lettering designed by Timmins himself, there was a limited number of 'large paper' copies for dedicated collectors. The publisher, Elliot Stock of London, had brought out Timmins's earlier volume, *Nooks and Corners of Herefordshire*, in 1892 and would go on to publish the last of the trilogy, *Nooks and Corners of Shropshire*, in 1899.

Nooks & Corners of Pembrokeshire was published by subscription. This was a popular method of publishing books for which the publisher was unsure of the demand. A prospectus announcing the intention to publish was distributed amongst likely buyers who were invited to register their interest in a copy or copies prior to publication. If sufficient subscribers were obtained the publication could go ahead and those who had showed their faith in the book had the satisfaction of finding their names listed for all to see in the list of subscribers.

These books are not solemn in their presentation of history, although Timmins always tried to be accurate in the information he gave. Rather did he intend the text to read easily and not to weigh too heavily on the reader. Above all, the text was a compliment to the illustrations which the author/artist took great trouble over. So successfully did Timmins manage the marriage of text and drawings in all three of his books that they were instant favourites in the three counties he chose to portray and have remained so ever since.

Timmins was a Birmingham man and, though he travelled a great deal, it was countryside not too distant from his midlands home that he set out to explore in the Nooks and Corners series. He had trained as an architect but gave up that profession to 'follow his strong bent for art'. His father, Frederick Timmins (no doubt the F.H. Timmins of Edgbaston in the list of subscribers), was a collector of what were known at the turn of the century as 'modern' watercolours, meaning David Cox and the like, and it is evident that the young Henry imbibed his love of art from an early age. Timmins and his wife travelled widely in England and abroad, extending their journeying to Egypt, India, Burma, and Ceylon. Lengthy visits to Italy and the countries of the south seem to have been frequent. There is not much evidence for Timmins' commercial activity as an artist although he was a contributor to the 'English Illustrated Magazine'. The frequency of his travels indicates that he was probably financially independent. Timmins does not appear to have published anything else. He died at Rome in 1908.

Paul Latcham
Hereford, September 1997

PUBLISHER'S NOTE

Nooks and Corners of Pembrokeshire was published originally with two folding maps: a facsimile of Speed's 1610 map of Pembrokeshire and a map of the county drawn by Timmins himself dated January 1895. Folding plates, costly things nowadays, would have added materially to the price of this reprint which is intended to reach the public at an affordable price. Regrettably, neither map would have been sufficiently legible to have any real significance if reduced to the page size of the book. Both maps have, therefore, been omitted. The book is otherwise complete as it first appeared including the list of subscribers.

PREFACE.

THE kindly reception accorded to my 'Nooks and Corners of Herefordshire,' both by the public and the press, has encouraged me (where, indeed, encouragement was little needed) to set forth anew upon my sketching rambles, and explore the Nooks and Corners of Pembrokeshire.

In chronicling the results of these peregrinations, I feel that I owe some apology to those whose knowledge of the Shire of Pembroke is far more thorough and intimate than my own, and upon whose preserves I may fairly be accused of poaching. I venture to plead, in extenuation, an inveterate love for exploring these unfrequented byways of my native land, and for searching out and sketching those picturesque old buildings that lend such a unique interest to its sequestered nooks and corners.

Pembrokeshire is rich in these relics of a bygone time, but for one reason or another they do not appear to have received the attention they certainly deserve. Few counties can boast anything finer of their kind than the mediæval castles of Pembroke, Manorbere and Carew; while St. Davids Cathedral and the ruined Palace of its bishops, nestling in their secluded western vale, form a scene that alone is worth a visit to behold. No less remarkable in their way are the wonderful old crosses, circles and cromlechs, which remind the traveller of a vanished race as he tramps the broad fern-clad uplands of the Precelly Hills. It is a notable fact that 'he who runs may read,' in the

b

diversified character of its place-names, an important and interesting chapter of Pembrokeshire history. The south-western portion of the county, with the Saxon 'tons' of its Teutonic settlers, is as English as Oxfordshire, and hence has acquired the title of 'Little England beyond Wales.' On the other hand, the northern and eastern districts are as Welsh as the heart of Wales; and there, as the wayfarer soon discovers for himself, the mother-tongue of the Principality is the only one 'understanded of the people.'

Although Pembrokeshire cannot pretend to lay claim to such striking scenery as the North Wallian counties display, yet its wind-swept uplands and deep, secluded dingles have a character all their own; while the loftier regions of the Precelly Hills, and the broken and varied nature of the seaboard, afford many a picturesque prospect as the traveller fares on his way.

In compiling the following notes I have availed myself of Fenton's well-known work on Pembrokeshire, and of the writings of George Owen of Hênllys; I have consulted the records of that prolific chronicler, Gerald de Barri; Bevan's 'History of the Diocese of St. Davids;' and Jones and Freeman's exhaustive work on St. Davids Cathedral; besides various minor sources of local information which need not be specified here.

In conclusion, I take this opportunity to tender my sincere thanks to those friends and acquaintances whose ready help and advice so greatly facilitated my task, while at the same time enhancing the pleasure of these sketching rambles amidst the Nooks and Corners of Pembroke-shire.

H. THORNHILL TIMMINS.

Harrow, 1895.

CONTENTS.

INDEX TO ILLUSTRATIONS.

NOOKS AND CORNERS OF PEMBROKESHIRE.

CHAPTER I.

A GENERAL SURVEY.   THE KING'S TOWN OF TENBY.

AWAY beyond the many-folding hills of Brecon and Glamorgan, whose hollow 'cwms' are seamed with smoke from many a pit and furnace: far away beyond the broad uplands and fertile straths where Towey and Teivy seek the sea; the ancient shire of Pembroke thrusts forth, against the western main, its bold and rugged coast-line. From Strumble Head to Caldey, the grim primæval rocks that guard these storm-beaten shores bear the full brunt of the Atlantic gales upon their craggy bastions; which, under the ceaseless influence of time and tempest, have assumed endless varieties of wild, fantastic outline and rich harmonious colouring.

A weather-beaten land is this, where every tree and hedgerow tells, in horizontal leeward sweep, of the prevalent 'sou'-wester.' Few hills worthy the name break these wide-expanded landscapes, above whose 'meane hills and dales' one graceful mountain range rises in solitary pre-eminence. Stretching athwart the northern portion of the county, the shapely peaks of the Precelly Mountains dominate every local prospect, attaining in Moel Cwm Cerwyn a height of 1,760 feet, and throwing out westwards the picturesque heights of Carn Englyn;

whence the range finally plunges seawards in the bold buttress of
Dinas Head, and the wild and rugged hills of Pencaer.

The inferior heights of Treffgarn and Plumstone 'mountain,'
whose singular crags recall the tors of Cornwall, form a quaint feature
in the prospect during the otherwise tedious drive to St. Davids.
Perched upon the westernmost spur of these hills, the lonely peel-tower
of Roch Castle looks out across the wind-swept plains of old Dewisland to the fantastic peaks of Carn Llidi and Pen-beri, whose ancient
rocks rise abruptly from the ocean.

Down from the broad, fern-clad shoulders of Precelly flow the few
Pembrokeshire streams that approach the dignity of rivers. Hence
the twin floods of Eastern and Western Cleddau, rising far asunder
at opposite ends of the range, meander southwards in widely-deviating
courses through the heart of the county, to unite beneath the walls of
Picton Castle, and merge at last into the tidal waters of Milford Haven.

Westwards flows the little river Gwaen, circling through a picturesque vale beneath the shadow of Carn Englyn, and emerging
from its secluded inland course upon the narrow, land-locked harbour
of Fishguard. Towards the north a group of streamlets unite to form
the Nevern River, which flows, amidst some of the most charming
scenery in the county, through the village of that ilk. After passing
beneath the luxuriant groves of Llwyngwair, the Nevern stream enters
a sandy bay and bears the modest commerce of Newport to the waterside hamlet of Parrog.

The Newgale Brook sweeps around Roch Castle, and enters
St. Bride's Bay through a broad rampart of shingle and sand. This
latter stream has from very early times formed the boundary between
the ancient provinces of Dewisland and Rhôs; and to this day the
Newgale Brook draws a line of demarcation between an English and
a Welsh speaking people. Upon its left bank lies Rhôs, a portion of
the district known as 'Little England beyond Wales,' with its Saxon
speech and Norman fortress of Roch; while all to westward stretches
venerable Dewisland, Welsh now as ever in tongue and in title.

The Solva River, emerging from a deep and narrow 'cwm,' forms one of the most picturesque harbours upon the coast—a tempting nook for the artist. Lastly, the little Allan Water, rising amidst those curious hills which overlook St. Davids, meanders past open, gorse-clad commons and marshlands abloom with the golden flag. Thenceforth the Allan winds around the ruins of the Bishop's palace, and finally loses itself in a tiny haven frequented by a few trading craft and small coastwise colliers.

Deep into the bluff outline of this sea-girt land, old Ocean encroaches by two important inlets of widely different character. As the wayfarer bound to St. Davids approaches his destination, the tedium of the long coach-drive is at last relieved by the welcome outlook across a broad expanse of sea. This is St. Bride's Bay, whose waters sweep inland past the ancient city for a distance of ten miles or so, having the large islands of Ramsey and Skomer lying upon either horn of the bay.

Tradition tells that, 'once upon a time,' a fair country studded with villages and farmsteads flourished where now the ocean rolls; and traces of submerged forests about Newgale, and elsewhere within the compass of the bay, suggest a possible grain of truth in the local fable.

A few miles farther down the coast the famous estuary of Milford Haven opens seaward between the sheltering heights of St. Anne's Head, and the long, crooked peninsula of Angle. Wonderful are the ramifications of this magnificent water-way, within whose spacious roadstead the whole British navy might with ease find anchorage; while its land-locked tidal reaches bear a modest local traffic to many a remote inland district, calling up memories of savours nautical beside the grass-grown quays of Pembroke and 'Ha'rfordwest.'

Well might Imogen marvel why Nature should have singled out 'this same blessed Milford' for such a priceless endowment, exclaiming:

'Tell me how Wales was made so happy as
To inherit such a Haven.'

The quaint author of 'Polyolbion' no less enthusiastically remarks:

'So highly Milford is in every mouth renown'd,
Noe Haven hath aught good, that in her is not found;'

while lastly, not to be outdone, George Owen, the old Pembrokeshire chronicler, declares his beloved 'Myllford Havon' to be the 'most famouse Porte of Christendome.'

Ever since those legendary days when St. Patrick sailed for the Emerald Isle upon the traditional millstone, this incomparable haven has continued to be a favourite point of departure for the opposite shores of Ireland ; and several historical personages appear at intervals in the annals of local events. Hence, for example, Henry II. sailed away upon his conquest of old Erin ; while in the Fourth Henry's reign a large body of French troops disembarked upon these shores, to co-operate in the wars of 'the irregular and wild Glendower.' Yet another famous individual, ycleped Henry ap Edmund ap Owain ap Meredydd ap Tydwr, better known as Henry Tudor, Earl of Richmond, landed at Milford Haven in the year of grace 1485, to set forth upon the historical campaign which won for him a crown on Bosworth field. Here, again, the ubiquitous Oliver Cromwell embarked with an army of some 15,000 men, to carry his victorious arms against the rebellious Irish ; and hence, in these piping times of peace, the mail-boats sail at frequent intervals to the seaports of the Emerald Isle.

Penetrating thus deeply into the country, one crooked arm of the great estuary 'creketh in' beneath the stately ruins of Carew Castle, in such wise as to partially 'peninsulate' a remote but interesting portion of South Pembrokeshire, which is still further isolated by the low range of the Ridgeway, between Pembroke and Tenby. This little district contains within its limited compass a wonderful variety of ruined castles, ancient priories, quaint old parish churches and curious, fortified dwelling-houses of the English settlers.

Nestling in the more sheltered hollows, or clinging limpet-like to the storm-swept uplands, these characteristic structures arouse the way-farer's interest as he paces the short, crisp turf rendered sweet by the driven sea-spray. Occasionally he will set his course by some promi-nent church steeple, which at the same time affords a landmark to the passing mariner as he sails around the wild and iron-bound headlands of the southern coast.

Throughout the length and breadth of Pembrokeshire, the constant recurrence of camps, cromlechs, hut-circles and other prehistoric remains, points to the existence of an extremely ancient people, whose origin is involved in the mists of unrecorded antiquity. These primæval monuments, seemingly old as the bleak hills they crown, suggest many an insoluble conundrum to the curious visitor, who, gazing in wonder upon their weatherbeaten yet indestructible masses, disposes of the archaic enigma as best he may by exclaiming: ' There were giants in those days !'

Coming down to the comparative *terra-firma* of historic times, we find, at the period of the Roman invasion, a Celtic race called the Demetæ dwelling in the district of which our county forms a portion. The masters of the world appear to have pushed their way to the western seaboard, where, according to tradition, they established their colony of Menapia beneath the shelter of the headland known to Ptolemy as Octopitarum ; connecting it, according to their custom, by the roadway of Via Julia with their base at Muridunum, or Carmarthen ; while the probably still older road, called Via Flandrica, or Fordd Fleming, afforded a route across the mountains to the north.

Taking another lengthy stride across the intervening centuries, we may trace the footsteps of the Norman invaders. Under the leadership of Arnulph de Montgomery, they overran these newly-conquered lands, and established themselves in those great strongholds of Pembroke, Manorbere, Carew, Haverfordwest and Roch, whose dismantled walls still dominate the surrounding country.

The wild Welsh proving inconveniently restive, that astute monarch Henry I. imported a colony of sturdy Flemings to assist in keeping order upon these distant marchlands ; an event which exerted a marked influence upon the course of local history. These thrifty settlers received further aid from the Second Henry, and settled down to cultivate the land wrested from the Celtic peasantry.

The natives, however, still continued to behave in a very unneigh-bourly fashion, ' making,' as we are told, ' verie sharpe warres upon the Flemings, sometimes with gaine, sometimes with losse ;' so that they were obliged to build for themselves those strong, fortified dwelling-houses whose massive remains are so frequently met with throughout the southern parts of the county.

In course of time the language of the immigrants superseded the ancient tongue of Celtic Dyfed, and thus that portion of the district comprised within the hundreds of Castlemartin and Rhôs acquired the title of 'Little England beyond Wales,' whose Saxon place-names, such as Johnston, Williamston, Hodgeston and the like, contrast so strikingly with the universal Llan-this, that and the other, still common throughout the upper country.

We have already had occasion to refer to Henry of Richmond's famous visit to Milford, and to recall the expeditions of Cromwell and other prominent personages from that noble haven to Ireland. The French 'invasion' of Wales in 1797 will be referred to in dealing with the scenes of that notorious exploit; and in the course of our narrative we shall touch upon various other historical incidents connected with the nooks and corners of this fascinating county.

Owing to the prevalence of westerly breezes from the open Atlantic, tempered by the beneficent influence of the Gulf Stream, Pembrokeshire is blessed with a mild and remarkably equable climate. Hence the air is at the same time both dry and bracing, particularly in the southern portion of the county, where, in sheltered situations, the myrtle, fuchsia and syringa flourish *al fresco* all the year round.

Nothing can exceed the luxuriance of the vegetation in the spacious demesne of Stackpole Court, where, sheltered from the strong winter gales that sweep across these gorse-clad uplands, the oak, ash, beech, ilex, sycamore and other forest trees, 'crowd into a shade' beside the lily-strewn meres whose placid waters mirror their spreading branches. This favoured region boasts, we believe, an average temperature of about 50° Fahr., and it has been shown by careful analysis that, taking one season with another, there is little to choose between the average climates of Madeira and of Tenby.

These favourable conditions do not, of course, obtain to the same degree in the north; where rough winds occasionally sweep down from the Precelly Mountains, driving keenly across the open country and retarding the vegetation. Nevertheless there are sheltered nooks around Newport and Fishguard where the eucalyptus, mulberry and fig-tree attain a goodly stature.

Sun-warmed spots such as these form, however, mere oases of verdure amidst the rolling, wind-swept uplands of the interior; where the hardier trees alone rear their stunted forms above the rough stone walls which serve in place of hedgerows, or cluster around a group of solid, one-storied cottages, whose low walls, deep roofs and vast, bulging chimneys are overspread with one universal coating of dazzling white-wash; 'to keep out the weather,' as the countryfolk will tell you—very clean, no doubt, but the reverse of picturesque in appearance.

The native style of building is well exhibited in the ancient parish churches, more especially in those towards the southern seaboard of the county, which are distinguished by a rugged simplicity entirely in keeping with the stern and sombre character of the surrounding land-scape. Of architecture there is but little; such beauty as the edifice can boast having to be sought in the picturesque grouping of its rambling gables beneath the tall, square, fortress-like tower; and the quaint, unlooked-for character of the cavernous interior.

The nave is frequently covered with a rude stone barrel vault, from which low vaulted transepts open out like cells on either hand, whence vast 'squints,' forming narrow passages, branch diagonally into the chancel. Low arches, sometimes pointed, sometimes of a curious flat shape and almost invariably devoid of mouldings, open into the aisles, which are lighted by lancet windows of simple but good design; while sometimes a roomy porch or handsome sedilia adds a touch of distinction to an otherwise homely interior.

We may instance, as typical examples of these sacred edifices, the churches of Gumfreston, St. Florence, Castlemartin and, *par excellence*, of Manorbere. A handsomer development may be studied in the parish churches of Tenby, Carew and Hodgeston, and the fine old priory church of Monkton. The graceful thirteenth-century pillars and arches of St. Mary's, Haverfordwest, are unusually ornate for this locality, and are only excelled by the varied and beautiful architecture of St. Davids Cathedral itself. There can be little doubt that the hard, intractable nature of the local limestone is in some degree responsible for the primitive characteristics of many of these churches; for, despite their archaic appearance, they are rarely older than early thirteenth-century times.

Beautiful in their decay are the time-honoured ruins of the episcopal palaces of Lamphey and St. Davids; whose mellow-toned walls with their singularly graceful arcades mark the constructive genius of Bishop Gower, the Wykeham of the West.

The numerous mediæval castles, whose ruined walls and ivy-mantled towers so frequently meet the eye, form a striking feature in many a picturesque scene; from the rugged bastions which cluster beneath the mighty keep of Pembroke, and the many-windowed front of lordly Carew, to the lonely peel-tower of Roch and the remote and isolated block-houses which keep ward around the coast.

Having thus obtained a general *coup d'œil* of our field of action, we will proceed to explore at our leisure the nooks and corners of this pleasant countryside; so, with this purpose in view, we now make our way to that highly-favoured watering-place, the 'King's town of Tenby.'

BECALMED OFF TENBY.

One clear, calm evening in May of this drouthy year of grace 1893, we emerge dusty and sun-baked from the tropical recesses of the 'tunnel express,' alight at Tenby Station, and wend our way through the streets of that clean little town to seaside quarters overlooking a

TENBY.

picturesque bay, where some fishing-craft lie quietly at anchor off the harbour mouth. Towards sundown a miniature fleet of trawlers sweeps gracefully landwards around the Castle Hill, looking for all the world like a flight of brilliant butterflies; their russet sails glowing in the warm light of the sun's declining rays with every hue from gold to ruddy purple, recalling memories of gorgeous scenes on far-away Venetian lagoons. Hailing from many a haven between Milford and strong-savoured Brixham, these handy little vessels ply their calling around our south-western shores; pushing their ventures, when opportunity serves, to the North Sea fishing-grounds, and even to the remoter shores of Scotland. The visitor curious in such matters soon learns to distinguish between the well-found Brixham trawler and the handy sloop from Milford, certain cabalistic letters painted upon the parti-coloured sails denoting the port where, according to custom, each boat is respectively registered.

Tenby town is in many respects happy in what a local historian quaintly terms its '·approximation.' Turning its back upon the quarter whence blow the strongest gales, and sheltered by the high ground of the Ridgeway, that part of the town most frequented by visitors faces south by east across the land-locked waters of Carmarthen Bay.

Hence a pleasant view is obtained of the opposite coast of Gower and the more distant highlands of North Devon; while Caldey Island lies like a breakwater against the waves of the open Channel. As shrewd old Leland observes: ' Tinbigh Town standith on a main Rokke, but not very hy; and the Severn Se so gulfith in about hit that, at the ful Se, almost the third part of the Toun is inclosid with water.'

Tenby can boast a fair sprinkling of good hotels and lodging-houses. The town is made further attractive as a place of residence by a well-appointed club, a circulating library, excellent public baths and a small museum of local interest. Last, but by no means least amongst its attractions, Nature has provided a broad expanse of firm, dry sands, much appreciated by children and bathers at holiday times.

With a fair train-service upon the railway, good carriages and boats for hire, and steamboats calling at intervals, Tenby affords a convenient centre whence to explore the remoter recesses of South

Pembrokeshire, for few and far between are the resting-places for the wayfarer in that rather inaccessible region.

Dynbych-y-Pysgod—the Little Town of Fish—appears to have been a place of some importance from very early times. By the middle of the twelfth century we find the town in the hands of the Flemish soldiery; and subsequently disasters came thick and threefold upon the devoted inhabitants. During the reign of Henry II., Maelgwyn ap Rhys, a person who is euphemistically described as 'of civil behaviour and honesty in all his actions,' ascertaining that many of the townsfolk were absent at the foreign wars, made a sudden onslaught, set fire to the ill-fated town, and burnt it to the ground. Less than a century later the place was again taken and destroyed by Llewelyn ap Grufydd; and after a further respite of about 200 years, the notorious Owain Glyndwr appeared before the walls, laid siege to, and made himself master of the little Western seaport.

Notwithstanding these misfortunes, 'the King's town of Tenby' henceforth grew and prospered unmolested. In 1402 Tenby was made a corporate town; and by the middle of the fifteenth century it had already become a centre of considerable trade and enterprise, encompassed by strong stone walls and towers built by Earl William de Valentia, Lord of Pembroke. The town walls are said to have been rebuilt by one Thomas White, the scion of a famous burgher family, who was Mayor of this ancient borough in 1457.

When Leland passed this way in the reign of bluff King Hal, he found the 'Toun strongeli waullid and well gatid, everi Gate having hys Port collis *ex solide ferro.*' 'But,' says Fenton, writing in the early part of the present century, 'it was left for Queen Elizabeth, who was a great benefactress of the town in general, and whose initials are still extant over parts of the town walls, to contribute that strength and perfection to them which the present remains are a striking proof of.' Earl William (who appears to have been a generous patron of the town) granted the first charter of liberties, which was afterwards renewed and confirmed by successive reigning sovereigns. Several of these interesting documents are still in the possession of the Corporation, including an illuminated charter of Richard III.'s reign, and another granted by Edward VI., which is enriched with a quaint, archaic portrait of that youthful monarch.

Tenby also boasts a handsome pair of silver maces, presented to the town by Charles II. They are about 2 feet in length, and are emblazoned with the royal arms, the arms of Tenby, and other appropriate devices, with the inscription 'Rice Borrow Maior, 1660.' The upper portion of the head is formed as a moveable lid, so that the mace could be used upon festive occasions as a loving-cup.

Since those turbulent days of its earlier career, Tenby has played the modest *rôle* of a town without a history, and has happily combined

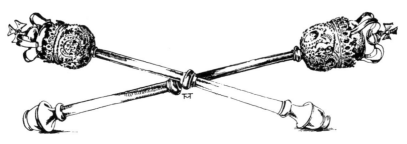

Maces Presented to Tenby by Charles II.

the avocations of a fishery town with the seductions of a modern watering-place.

Turning out into the steadfast sunshine, we now thread our way amid the intricacies of the older byways to the 'faire Paroche chirche,' whose steeple, soaring high aloft, appears a landmark to mariners far out at sea. Dedicated to St. Mary, this church is one of the largest and handsomest in the county, and is unrivalled in the beauty and interest of its monuments.

Foremost amongst these are the twin marble monuments in St. Anne's Chapel, which figure in the foreground of our sketch. Here lie buried several distinguished members of that famous family, the Whites of Tenby, which has given many worthy citizens to the town.

Beneath the right-hand tomb rests Thomas White, merchant and sometime Alderman of Tenby; whose recumbent effigy, habited in the distinctive costume of his calling, adorns the monument. He it was who enabled Henry, Earl of Richmond, to escape after the battle of Tewkesbury, by concealing him in his house at Tenby until such time as he could ship him safely off in one of his own vessels to France. In gratitude for this yeoman service the Earl, upon his accession to the

The Chancel of
St. Mary's Church
Tenby

throne, presented his trusty friend with the lease of all the Crown lands around the town.

The adjacent monument, which closely resembles its neighbour, records another member of the White family. Both these tombs are enriched with figures, in panels of bold relief, with a running inscription in mediæval character carved upon the margin.

Our attention is next attracted by the gaily-tinted effigy of William Risam, who, clad in aldermanic robes, kneels beneath a canopy built into the chapel wall. The figure is coloured in such a life-like manner that, as the story goes, a Parliamentarian soldier fired at the supposed enemy; in witness whereof a bullet-hole may be discerned above the head of the effigy.

Near at hand lies the last of that ancient family the Vaughans, of Dunraven in South Wales; a man who, having run through his patrimony at breakneck pace, allowed the ancestral mansion to fall into ruin, and betook himself to a lonely turret upon the seaward cliffs. Here he is said to have spent his time in showing false lights along the coast, in order to lure passing vessels ashore and enrich himself by the plunder of their cargoes. One stormy night, during one of these sinister exploits, the body of his only son was washed ashore at his feet; when, overcome by this ominous catastrophe, he quitted the neighbourhood, withdrew from all intercourse with his fellow-creatures, and ended his days in seclusion at Tenby.

Standing upon the chapel floor hard by, we espy a fine old fifteenth-century church bell bearing in black-letter characters the words SANCTA ✠ ANNA, with the initials R. T. This is the ancient sanctus-bell of this same chapel of St. Anne, which has descended to its present lowly position from the exterior of the tower, having been hung there, as is supposed, long years ago by Thomas ap Rhys, of Scotsborough, a descendant of the famous Rhys ap Thomas who played so important a part in the establishment of Henry VII. upon the throne. The memory of this worthy knight is kept evergreen by the gaudy and rather pretentious-looking monument seen on the farther wall. There he kneels, with folded hands, arrayed in ruffles and trunk-hose; his 'better half,' who is represented as of gigantic proportions, reposing uncomfortably upon her side; while in panels beneath appear the sons and daughters, arranged in symmetrical gradation. A glance at the sketch will show the pretty contrast afforded by the diversified forms of the arches; while the lofty flight of steps ascending to the chancel, and the dark timbers of the roof supported by well-carved angels upon massive brackets, enhance the effect of the handsome interior.

Quitting the church by its massive south porch, we pause beneath the spreading elms that adorn the churchyard to admire a singular group of arches, set in a crumbling fragment of ruined wall, whose gray, time-worn stones are abloom with bright tufts of pink valerian. These appear to be the sole remains of a house of Carmelite nuns, established

A.D. 1399 by one John de Swyne-more; and so graceful are these richly-moulded arches that we can but regret that more of the structure has not been spared to us. It is probable that these ruins are of cöeval date with the adjacent western doorway of the church, which has a peculiar ogee arch surmounted with the following inscription in Gothic characters: BENEDICTUS DEUS IN DONIS SUIS.

Rambling haphazard around the little town, such names as Frog Street, Crackwell Street and the like, tickle our fancy as a quaint relief to modern street nomenclature, which, usually devoid of originality, too often supplants local names racy of the soil.

A BIT OF OLD TENBY.

A sudden turn down a narrow lane, hanging, as it were, upon the steep hillside, reveals glimpses of old-world Tenby which beguile our wandering steps from the hard highway.

At a secluded corner of these by-lanes a gray and weather-beaten old house stands, forsaken and neglected, amid the meaner dwellings that encompass it. The well-proportioned windows and pointed door-way which adorn the massive front lend a certain air of faded dignity, as though the old place had once 'seen better days'; while above the high-pitched roof peers one of those curious, rounded erections called hereabouts ' Flemish ' chimneys.

In conjunction with the ancient gables at the rear of the adjacent saddler's shop, this interesting old structure forms one of the most picturesque relics yet remaining of the Tenby of ' auld lang syne.'

Following hence the groups of stalwart fisher-folk as, with large air of leisure, they stroll adown the hill, we soon find ourselves upon the ' Peere made for Shyppes ' which encloses the little harbour. Here stood in olden times the seamen's chapel of St. Julian, which was

RUINS OF
ST. MARYS PRIORY
AT TENBY.

subsequently converted into a bath-house : thus ' cleanliness comes next to godliness '; and a pretty modern chapel now stands beside the quay.

Close at hand, in a sheltered cove, the lifeboat lies in wait beside a rudimentary iron ' peere,' which threatens to stretch its spindle shanks athwart the comely crescent of the bay, beneath the fortress-crowned islet of St. Catherine.

The adjacent Castle Hill is crowned by a lofty watch-tower, some ruined outworks of the ancient city walls, and a handsome marble statue of the late Prince Consort, of heroic size : lower down stands

3

a small but well-arranged museum, which contains a representative collection of local natural history, besides valuable cases of shells, coins, etc.

OLD HOUSES AT TENBY

Archæologists will notice with interest the small alabaster group of St. George and the Dragon, rescued from a cottage in course of demolition at Tenby; and a fine specimen of a quern, used for grinding corn, found near Popton. The exterior is fashioned into the form of a human face, and as it is known that only the earlier examples were ornamented, this quern is considered to be of very high antiquity.

The seaward face of the hill is laid out in winding walks, with sheltered seats at intervals, where visitors and townsfolk congregate upon the sunny slopes to indulge in a spell of *dolce far niente*, or to enjoy the wide panorama of land and sea that lies outspread around.

The return to the town may be varied by strolling along the broad, firm sands beneath curiously contorted rocky cliffs, aglow just now with masses of the white and red valerian. Clambering up a long flight of steps, we soon find ourselves abreast of the massive walls which in olden times protected the town upon its landward side, and terminated upon the precipitous edge of the cliff in the quaint, ivy-clad tower that rises right here before us.

These ancient walls are still (in spite of hard treatment in bygone times from vandalistic hands) in a fair state of preservation; and form, with their boldly-projecting towers and broken battlements, the most

striking and picturesque feature of the town.   They are perhaps seen
to the best advantage from near the north-west corner, whence a general
coup d'œil is gained of their respective sides.

Sauntering under the shady trees on the site of the ancient moat,
we pass beside the south-west front, to which, as by far the most complete, we now devote our attention.   Here we notice how the sturdy
round tower which guards the converging angle spreads boldly out at

S⁺ GEORGES GATE, TENBY.

its base; anon we observe another tower of similar form, through which
the easy-going authorities of some past time have actually permitted a
huge opening to be hewn to admit the passage of a ropewalk !

A stone's-throw farther on rises the broad bulk of the great
St. George's Bastion, marking the entrance to one of the principal
town gates, and pierced with five archways, in two of which the grooves
for the portcullis may still be discerned.   Overhead a gangway ran
around the inner face of the wall, which is provided with lancet-holes

for the use of archers, and is crowned with the usual corbelled battle-ments. Altogether this fine old structure presents a most picturesque appearance; its ancient archways being frequently enlivened by groups of market folk passing to and fro, while the rough gray stones of its venerable walls are wreathed with masses of flowering plants. A number of shabby dwellings which encumbered the approach have recently been swept away; one dilapidated old building with curious circular chimneys (said to have been used as a lazar-house) alone being spared.

Beyond St. George's Bastion rises another ivy-mantled tower, near which we espy a stone panel let into the wall, bearing the superscription 'Aᵒ 1588, E. R.' Being interpreted, this inscription records that Tenby walls were repaired in the thirtieth year of good Queen Bess's reign.

Farther on the wall is pierced with a wide open archway, and terminates abruptly upon the precipitous edge of the cliff in a square, battlemented turret bearing a strong family likeness to the church towers of this locality. The walls seem to have been pierced with a double row of lancet-holes for the use of archers, the upper tier being commanded by a gangway carried upon pointed arches, while the lower row is accessible from the ground.

The day waxing warm and sunny, we now make for the harbour again, and charter one of the numerous well-found pleasure-boats which lie in wait for visitors. An hour's pleasant sail over a sea blue as the Mediterranean, and we land upon the shores of Caldey Island, like the Old Man of the Sea, pick-a-back fashion astride the boatman's back.

'This island,' says George Owen, 'is verie fertile and yeldeth plentie of corne; all their plowes goe with horses, for oxen the inhabitantes dare not keepe, fearing the purveyors of the pirattes as they themselves told me, whoe often make their provisions there by theire owne comission, and comonlie to the good contentment of the inhabitantes, when conscionable theefes arrive there.'

A grassy track, winding up the sloping bank amidst gorse and bracken, now leads across a stream and beside a few quarrymen's cottages to a dejected-looking chapel. In a neglected corner of the interior we discover the object of our visit—to wit, a recumbent oblong stone inscribed with certain archaic characters, which have been rendered as follows: ' In the Name both of the Cross itself and of Him who was fixed thereon, pray for the soul of Catuoconus.' Certain lines of the character known as Ogham may also be discerned upon the sides or edges of this hoary monolith.

The Priory.
. Caldy Island

Striking across the open fields, with the tall white lighthouse for our guide, we turn aside to visit an old farmstead that contains the scanty ruins of Caldey Priory. This venerable foundation owes its origin to Robert, son of Martin de Turribus, and was annexed as a cell to the abbey of St. Dogmaels, near Cardigan.

A wise old saw which observes ' There is nothing new but what has been forgotten,' may find a verification amidst such neglected nooks as these; whose long-forgotten relics of a bygone age greet the wayfarer with all the charm of novelty.

Above the adjacent farmyard premises rises the quaint little weather-beaten tower of the old priory chapel; its slender spire leaning perilously awry, its stonework fast crumbling to decay. From the summit of the tower hangs the crazy bell, with rusty chain and silent clapper. One daintily-fashioned window is roughly blocked with brickwork, another gives entrance to a pigeon-cot.

Within the adjoining house we are shown a fine old vaulted kitchen, with deep-browed windows, and rude stone settle along the wall. Thence we penetrate to a cool, dark chamber exhibiting traces of a gracefully proportioned window enclosed by a pointed arch, long since blocked up.

Retracing our steps beneath hedges of flowering fuchsia, we return by breezy, fern-clad commons and well-tilled fields to the landing-place; where an amphibious-looking individual is laying out lobster-pots among the weed-strewn rocks.

Caldey has ever been famed for the excellence of its oyster fisheries; not to speak of the crabs and lobsters caught around its rocky shores, which are commended by an Elizabethan writer who appears to have been an authority on such matters. 'The Lapster,' says this enthusiast, 'sett whole on the table, yieldeth Exercise, Sustenance and Contemplation; exercise in cracking his legs and Clawes, sustenance by eating the Meate thereof, and contemplation by beholding the curious Work of his complete Armour, both in hue and workmanship.'

'And the Crabbe,' continues the same writer, 'doth sensiblye feele the Course of the Moone; fillinge and emptyeing yt selfe with the encrease and decrease thereof, and therefore ys saied to be best at the full Moone.'

Once more afloat, we are speedily wafted past the cave-pierced cliffs of St. Margaret's Isle, and across the placid waters of Caldey Sound. Running beneath the fortress-crowned St. Catherine's Rock, we round the Castle Hill and disembark in Tenby's sheltered haven.

Though our rambles about its old streets have by no means exhausted the curious nooks of Tenby, yet we have all broad Pembrokeshire lying as it were at our doors, and waiting only for an 'open sesame' to disclose its most interesting features. By far the larger number of these lie within a measurable distance of Tenby, whence access is easily obtained to them by road, rail, or boat. Moreover, by taking counsel with the local time-table, the visitor may fare forth upon his way at a conscionable hour of the morning and be back again at Tenby ere nightfall supervenes.

The curious old chest figured at the foot of this chapter formed the ancient treasury of Tenby. It is enriched with sixteenth-century German ironwork of very quaint design—witness the ladies pulling the elephants' ' noses,'—and has seven bolts and two padlocks.   The keys of these latter were held by the two town bailiffs, while the Mayor was responsible for those of the main lock and of the tiller inside.   After having been sold as old iron some five-and-thirty years ago, this interesting relic was rescued by a Tenby resident, through whose courtesy we are enabled to show the accompanying sketch.

THE ANCIENT TREASURY OF TENBY.

CHAPTER II.

ROUND ABOUT THE RIDGEWAY.

' The year's at the spring
  And day's at the dawn ;
Morning's at seven ;
  The hillside's dew-pearled ;
The lark's on the wing ;
  The snail's on the thorn :
God's in the heaven—
  All's right with the world !'
                    R. B.

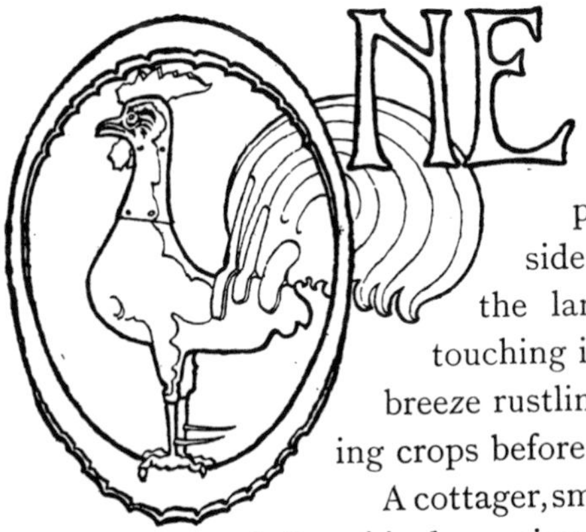

FINE May morning, after a night of soft, seasonable rain, we are up betimes and away into the green borderland that encompasses Tenby town upon its western side. Low, hazy clouds drift athwart the landscape, with glints of sunlight touching it into life here and there ; a gentle breeze rustling the trees and bowing the growing crops before it.

A cottager, smoking a morning pipe on the bench before his door, gives us the *sele* of the day as we pass, and would fain spin a yarn about the 'craps' and the drought ; but, turning a deaf ear to his lucubrations, we go our ways rejoicing, and ere long find ourselves skirting a lush green tract of marshland, whose dark levels are gay with yellow flags, marsh marigolds and feathery 'ragged Robin.'

Diverging to the right and plunging into a grove of aged ash-trees, we soon emerge upon an open glade where stand the crumbling walls of

4

an ancient house called Scotsborough. This was the ancestral home of the family of Ap Rhys, who repose in Tenby Church beneath the monument we have already visited ; and a ramble amidst the intricate passages and loopholed chambers of the ruined mansion, with their huge chimneys and cavernous ovens, shews that it was erected at a time when a man's house still continued to do duty, at a pinch, as his castle. Having explored this picturesque old pile, we hark back once more to the road. Trudging along a hollow, shady lane past a pretty mill, we now strike into a secluded pathway which drops steeply down beside a prattling rill, beneath overarching trees whose interlacing branches fret the greensward with a mantle of shadowy verdure.

Overhead the fleecy clouds are swept by the breeze into graceful forms suggestive of sea-birds' wings ; while the sunny air is musical with the song of birds and the distant bleating of sheep, and sweet with the scent of chestnut and elder bloom. A newly-fledged Burnet butterfly tries his smart speckled wings ; whilst a passing 'Blue' out- rivals the hue of the dainty speedwell in the hedgerow ; which peeps from amidst a tangle of pushing young bracken, hooded 'lords and ladies,' bluebells and wild geranium.

Here in this secluded nook, 'the world forgetting, by the world forgot,' nestles the venerable church of Gumfreston ; its ivy-mantled tower scarce rivalling the lofty trees which screen it from the outer world. Approached by footpaths only, a rustic wicket gives access to the churchyard ; crossing which we enter the lowly edifice by an arched doorway that opens into a roomy old porch of primitive construction, completely overgrown with ivy. This was in all probability the original church, and is entirely built of stone ; the roof, after the manner of the older churches of the district, being fashioned into a simple kind of vault. Upon either side is a rude stone bench ; and a stoup, or font, of archaic design is built into the wall.

Passing through the inner door, some slight traces of damaged fresco which appear upon the whitewashed wall may, by a vigorous exercise of the imagination, be conjectured to represent the martyrdom of St. Lawrence, the patron saint of Gumfreston Church. Something roughly resembling a tennis-racket may pass for the martyr's gridiron ; while a gigantic foot, and certain objects vaguely suggesting a pair of scissors and a comb, are faintly discernible amidst a number of other half-obliterated details.

A curious recess which bulges outwards from the same wall con-

tains an old stone font ; and the small adjacent transept is connected with the chancel by one of those singular ' squint ' passages peculiar to this locality.

An unusual effect is produced by the low, simple arch—scarce more than 5 feet wide—between the chancel and the nave, which has a shallow, pointed recess on either side of it, doubtless designed to hold figures.

In one of these latter we observe the primitive-looking pewter flagon and paten which serve the purpose of church plate. Alongside them stands a queer little cracked handbell of bronze-green, rust-eaten metal; this is the Sanctus-bell which, in pre-Reformation days, was rung in the church upon the elevation of the Host, and was carried at the head of funeral processions. Anent its present damaged condition the story goes that, during some solemn rite of exorcism with bell, book and candle, a certain fallen potentate suddenly appeared in a flash of brimstone flame, and broke the bell in impotent revenge.

Passing through the chancel, we now enter a quaint little side-chapel with pretty two-light window and low, groined ceiling whose stony ribs look strong enough to carry a tower. The latter, however, is on the other side of the church, and is probably of later date; it is built in several stages, the one below the bell-chamber having pigeon-holes around inside the walls; while overhead hangs an ancient bell inscribed SANCTA MARIA ORA PRO NOBIS.

CHURCH PLATE
AT CUMFRESTON.

Hard by the church upon its southern side a flight of worn, stone steps leads down to three clear springs, which well up side by side in a mossy dell, and ripple away beneath lush grasses and flowering marsh plants. These wells, although in such close proximity, have been found to differ in their medicinal properties; and were resorted to as a cure for ' all the ills that flesh is heir to ' by the simple folk of a bygone generation.

Near at hand is the site of an old cockpit. In days of yore this exhilarating sport was very popular with Pembrokeshire men, who usually chose Easter Monday and such-like ' times of jollitie ' to indulge in their favourite pastime.

At the corner of the churchyard stands an old deserted cottage which, after many vicissitudes, has fallen upon degenerate days. Originally the rectory, and then the poor-house of the parish, it is now a neglected ruin half hidden amidst a tangle of shrubs and climbing plants.

Most visitors to Gumfreston will notice the fine old farmhouse that rises cheek-by-jowl with the carriage-road from Tenby. If we are to believe the tradition of the countryside, this is the most ancient abode in the county. Be that as it may, the place bears traces of no mean antiquity; and is an excellent specimen of a Pembrokeshire homestead of the olden times.

Out from the main structure projects a mighty porch, running up the full height of the house, and pierced with round holes by way of windows above the main doorway. Penetrating into the interior, we enter a low-browed kitchen with open raftered ceiling and roomy settle beside the cavernous fireplace; its solid old timbers worn to a fine polish by generations of rustic shoulders. A bright wood-fire burns on the open hearth, and over it a big black kettle swings in the hollow of the chimney.

The chimney stacks cropping boldly out, haphazard as it were, lean independently this way or that in the quaintest way imaginable; and the broad gable ends are pierced with many pigeon-holes. The place is built as though intended to last for all time, and is enveloped in the customary coating of weather-stained whitewash.

We now push merrily on beneath a cloudless sky; meeting an exhilarating sea-breeze as the road mounts upwards. Luxuriant hedge-rows (a rare sight hereabouts) presently give place to open downland, affording widespreading views across rich, rolling woodlands cropped close by the strong salt breezes. Upon the broad slopes of the Ridge-way groups of white farm-buildings sparkle amidst ruddy ploughfields; while far beyond them are Caldey Island and the pale blue line of the sea.

Once more a pleasant fieldpath beguiles our errant footsteps. Leading across an open common, it presently drops into a narrow by-lane, which winds among hazel copses and undergrowth beside the marshy course of the Ritec, where cattle are browsing leisurely, half hidden amidst lusty water-plants.

Anon our lane degenerates into a hollow watercourse fringed with the greenest of mosses and wineglass ferns; insomuch that, like Agag, we are compelled to walk delicately across the rough stepping-stones that here do duty as a footpath; while the hedgerows fairly meet over-head in a tangle of wild roses, hawthorn and fragrant honeysuckle.

Emerging all too soon upon the dusty highway, we approach the pretty village of St. Florence. Being by this time not a little 'sharp set,' we enter a modest wayside inn, and proceed to whet our appetites upon the rations that the *gute verständige Hausfrau* soon sets before us. Let us unfold our simple bill of fare: New-laid eggs galore; a mighty loaf of likely-looking bread, sweet from the clean wood oven; and a draught of the 'cup that'—in moderation—'cheers, but not in-ebriates.'

In one corner of the low-ceiled room, the glass panels of an old-fashioned cupboard reveal a heterogeneous collection of rustic crockery-ware. The narrow mantel-board is adorned with a curious centrepiece, representing Wesley preaching to a sham china clock. This *chef d'œuvre* is supported on either hand by china figures, rather the worse for wear, riding to market upon a pillion; of which the rickety mirror behind renders a dull and distorted replica.

From the opposite wall the bucolic face of a former proprietor stares stonily out upon us, as he grasps his doll-like daughter's arm after the manner of a pump-handle; this interesting group being flanked by the inevitable memorial cards to lost ones long since 'buried.'

Meanwhile, as we ply the peaceful calumet, mine hostess tells of quaint old customs that, until only the other day, survived in this quiet countryside. 'I mind the time,' says she, 'when I was a girl, when there used to be a Vanity Fair in the village every Michaelmas tide. It lasted three whole days, and the men and maids would turn out in their best then, and all the housen must be smartened up and put in order; and Squire, he give every working man in the place a bran-new suit of clothes to his back. Ah, there was fine doings then, and I've a-hard tell that they'd used to run a keg of spirits, or what not, from the big cellars down Tenby way. But that was afore my time.'

A stroll around the village reveals some picturesque corners here and there; a few of the older cottages retaining the vast rounded chimneys, bulging ovens and pointed doorways of an earlier age. The church, too, contains attractive features. A peep into the little edifice reveals a curious vaulted interior, with its queer 'squint' passage set askew, and flat limestone arches of peculiar form on either side of the chancel.

The honours of the place are done by a garrulous old dame, whose russet-apple complexion, set amidst well-starched frills above a home-spun 'whittle,' shows how well she has weathered her fourscore hard-working winters.

Upon the gable wall outside, we notice a memorial slab commemo-rating a venerable couple who attained the mellow ages of 102 and 104, respectively; and a singular epitaph on Archdeacon Rudd: while the broken shaft of an ancient cross rises amidst the well-tended monuments of this flowery God's acre.

On our return to Tenby we pass a ruined water-mill, standing in a wooded dingle beside a reed-grown stream. Lanes and fieldpaths lead us down the valley of the Ritec, beside a group of tumbled houses whose massive, ivy-wreathed walls, with their narrow loopholed windows, may possibly guard those big cellars of which we have lately 'a-hard tell.'

Thence through a hollow dingle, where golden Fritillary butterflies float to and fro in the dappled sunlight; and where the fast-disappear-ing badger may still at times be met with. Anon we diverge to Cars-wall, to examine a group of remarkable stone buildings with vaulted chambers, huge fireplaces and bulging chimneys—puzzling objects to the archaeologist. From Carswall we strike across upland pastures, where a farm lad is 'tickling' the ruddy soil with a primitive kind of harrow, composed of a bundle of brushwood drawn behind a horse.

Erelong we turn aside to explore the recesses of Hoyle's Mouth; a vast cavern worn deep in the solid limestone of the Ridgeway, and fringed with fantastic stalactites resembling gigantic icicles. Relics of remote antiquity, discovered here, prove that the cavern has been a place of refuge in times beyond tradition; and a local fable affirms that it is connected with that 'mervellows caverne,' yclept the Wogan, far away beneath the Castle of Pembroke!

Half a mile hence, in a nook of the hill, stands the old farmhouse of Trefloyne; erstwhile the abode of a loyal family who, during Civil War times, paid the penalty of their constancy by being hunted forth by the Parliamentary soldiers; while their home was delivered over to destruction.

Another half-hour's walk takes us back to Tenby by way of Windpipe Lane; where a marble tablet by the roadside marks the site of St. John's Well, for many generations the sole water supply of the inhabitants. 'One thinge,' says Leland, 'is to be merveled at; there is no Welle yn the Towne, yt is said; whereby they be forced to fesh theyre Water from Saint Johns without ye Towne.' Nowadays, however, they have changed all that; and have provided a water supply more suited to modern requirements.

In the early days of the century, considerable ruins of the ancient Hospital of St. John still existed near this spot; of which, however, every trace has since been quite obliterated.

Another pleasant excursion from Tenby takes the visitor past the little secluded creek of Waterwinch; giving him, *en route*, a charming glimpse of the town, rising above the wooded shores of the north bay. Thence a steep, narrow lane leads to the village of Saundersfoot, a favourite seaside resort with a diminutive harbour, an hotel and groups of lodging-houses.

The whole of this district has been, at some remote geological period, one vast forest, of which traces still exist upon the adjacent coast; where submerged trees, and balks of timber encrusted with shells, are occasionally found. Tall chimney-shafts, rising amidst the woods, attest the presence of anthracite coal beneath our feet; this is raised from several mines in the neighbourhood, and sent down by tramway to Saundersfoot for exportation.

Pursuing a delightfully shady road that winds inland past the grounds of Hean Castle, we soon find ourselves amidst some of the loveliest sylvan scenery in all the countryside. Presently we get a peep at the church of St. Issels, almost lost to view amidst green aisles of embowering foliage.

As at Gumfreston, by footpaths only can the little edifice be approached; while the stepping-stones across the rivulet are supplemented by a rustic foot-bridge, for use in times when the stream is in flood. This church has lately been restored by some appreciative hand; it has the characteristic tall gray tower such as we have grown accustomed to in this locality, and contains a handsome font of respectable antiquity.

Hence the wayfarer may return to Tenby by way of Bonville's Court, a fortified manor-house of the Edwardian period, of which but a single dilapidated tower and stair-turret remain: or by fetching a compass round, and wandering through quiet lanes draped with harts-tongue fern, ivy and convolvulus, he may explore the country away towards Jeffreyston or Redberth; returning over high ground beside the finely-timbered estate of Ivy Tower; and so home by the previously mentioned route through Gumfreston village.

* * * * *

Nestling in a sunny nook where the Ridgeway meets the sea, the little village of Penally, peeping coyly out from amidst embowering trees, forms a pretty feature in many a local prospect.

The road, winding inland, leads us by a long causeway across a broad tract of marshland, now golden with iris and kingcups, through which the Ritec stream meanders to the sea. It is said that, in ancient times, the tidal waters extended up this hollow vale as far as the village of St. Florence; and there is an old map at Tenby in which a vessel in full sail floats upon the very spot where we now stand.

Thence up we climb again across the foot-hills of the Ridgeway, until ere long the first cottages of Penally ' heave in sight,' bowered in roses, clematis and honeysuckle, and set amidst gardens aglow with gladiolus, peonies, tulips, geraniums, fuchsias and Japan lilies. Was

5

it not Washington Irving who remarked that we English had, in our country gardens, 'caught the coy and furtive graces of Nature, and spread them, like witchery, around these rural abodes'?

Before us lies a stretch of open greensward, shaded by groups of oak and hawthorn, whence rises the gray tower of the parish church; a building which has been restored to a semblance of newness that belies its venerable traditions.

The interior has a pair of the now familiar 'squint' passages, a

few old tombs and a good stone font; and, *mirabile dictu*, is provided with the electric light. For this valuable innovation the village is indebted to Clement Williams, Esq., Mayor of Tenby, whose pretty country residence stands just above the church. Beneath the over-shadowing trees in the churchyard stands a finely carved early Celtic cross, similar to those found in Ireland; of which we shall see an even handsomer specimen when visiting Carew.

In former days Penally was held in high veneration, from a tradition that the miracle-working bones of St. Teilo, Bishop of Llandaff, rested here during their progress through the district.

A curious incident occurred here many years ago. During a fox-hunt in the vicinity, Reynard, being hard pressed by the hounds, sought refuge upon the roofs of some old farm buildings near the church. Here he led his pursuers a lively chase, but was eventually brought to earth and captured after an unusually exciting run.

We now push on for the wild scenery of the rocky coast overlooking Caldey Sound; pursuing a rough, sandy track amidst stretches of golden gorse.

The springy turf underfoot is literally tapestried with wild thyme, herb-Robert and thrift; over which butterflies, brown and azure-blue, float to and fro in the warm, still air; while from the radiant sky the lark's bright song falls pleasantly upon our ears. Hereabouts one must needs keep one's 'weather eye' open, to elude a tumble among the countless rabbit-holes that form pitfalls on every hand, whence the startled denizens scamper briskly to cover from beneath our very noses.

Presently we approach the secluded haven of Lydstep, and obtain a glimpse of the noble headland called Proud Giltar, whose red-brown cliffs rise sheer from the blue waves, with Caldey Island lying in the middle distance.

Traversing the pebbly beach, we pass near to Lydstep Point, a picturesque headland curiously scarped by disused limestone quarries. We now strike inland beneath a grove of trees growing in a sheltered corner, and ascend a narrow lane to a lonely cottage at the head of the glen. Hence we plunge down a deep, rocky ravine, whose seaward face is honeycombed with the caverns for which the place is famous.

Before us, league upon league, an ocean of purest blue spreads to the remote horizon; its sunny plain shimmering beneath white summer cloudlets, and empurpled by a thousand transient shadows. Huge rocks crop out on every hand from amidst the tangle of luxuriant under-growth that conceals the entrance to the Smugglers' Cave, a name we leave to tell its own wild tale of bygone times. Onward we scramble, down to the 'beachèd margent' of the shallow bay; whence a scene of rare beauty is beheld.

From the unsullied strand vast buttresses and pinnacles of lichen-clad limestone rise sheer and inaccessible; their solid ribs pierced with shadowy caverns wide as a cathedral vault and dark as Erebus, which tempt the wanderer to explore their deep, unknown recesses. Crystal-clear pools, fringed with dainty seaweeds and gemmed with starfish and sea-anemones, nestle in every hollow of the rocky shore; while shells of various tints encrust the untrodden sands.

Countless sea-birds wheel to and fro in the shadow of the cliffs, which echo their discordant cries as they clamour above the heads of the unwelcome intruders. Dusky cormorants scud with necks outstretched athwart the sparkling waves, while kittiwakes and guillemots crowd shoulder to shoulder upon the inaccessible ledges.

An hour is pleasantly spent groping amidst the hollows of a re-sounding cavern, or peering into the jewelled depths of some rocky sea-pool; or, anon, watching the plash of the translucent waves. At length, hungry as hawks, we beat a retreat to a sheltered nook amongst the rocks, to discuss *con gusto* our *al-fresco* lunch.

Fascinated by these entrancing prospects, we linger in this wonder-land until the advancing tide hints at a speedy departure, when, scrambling once again to the upper world, we strike away for the solitary hamlet of Lydstep.

Hard by the road stand two scattered groups of dilapidated build-ings, sometimes called by the imposing titles of the Palace, and the Place of Arms. In the good old times—so runs the legend—Aircol Llawhir, King of Dyfed, held his royal Court at this place.

Be that as it may, the existing structures are probably not older than the fourteenth century, and may be ascribed to those yeomen proprietors, a 'peg' above the common farmer folk, who erected these stout walls to safeguard their goods and chattels.

The return journey lies along a pleasant, open road between the Ridgeway and the cliffs; affording lovely glimpses of the rugged coastline and the land-locked sea. At Penally a return train puts in a timely appearance, and conveys us in a few minutes back to quarters, while the declining sun sets the world aflame in the glow of its lingering rays.

   *   *   *   *   *

 There is a spring-like feeling in the crisp morning air as we drive leisurely along the Ridgeway road, bound westward ho! to 'fresh woods and pastures new.'

 Fairy cobwebs, gemmed with glistening dewdrops, sparkle in every hedgerow as we mount slowly up the steep, ruddy flank of the Ridgeway. Bowling merrily along the smooth, well-kept road that traverses its breezy summit, we are in all probability following the course of some primitive trackway, used from the earliest times when enemies lurked in the lowlands.

 Ever wider grows the outlook as we jaunt along; the glory of the scene culminating as we clamber up the last of these steep 'pinches,' and call a halt, near a farm called the Rising Sun, to scan the summer landscape spread around.

 Close at hand broad meadows, green with the promise of spring, spread away down a winding valley tufted with shadowy woodlands, whence gray old steeples peep above the clustering cottage roofs. Far away amidst the folding hills, the walls and towers of lordly Carew rise near a silvery sheet of water—an arm of Milford Haven—backed by leagues of unexplored country, o'ertopped by the faint blue line of the Precelly Mountains—a glorious scene indeed!

> ' Ah ! world unknown ! how charming is thy view,
> Thy Pleasures many, and each pleasure new !'

 Turning across the lane, we lean upon a neighbouring gate, and leisurely scan the fair prospect over land and sea. Yonder the snow-white cottages gleam amidst the ruddy ploughlands. Seawards, the gorse-clad downs plunge in warm red sandstone cliffs to the all-encircling ocean, that stretches in unbroken span from St. Govan's Head, past Caldey Isle, to the gray-blue line of distant Devon, with Lundy lying under its lee.

 Forward again, betwixt pleasant greenswards tangled with fragrant gorse, brambles and unfurling bracken, within whose cool retreats the yellow-hammer lurks in his new spring bravery; while smart little goldfinches hunt in pairs amidst the thistle-heads under the hedgerow.

Gradually we slant away downwards, passing an ancient tumulus whence, in the old war times, a beacon fire gave warning against threatened invasion; and catching glimpses ahead of ruined towers and curtain-walls, where time-honoured old Pembroke nods over its memories of 'the days that are no more.' Soon we are clattering through the diminutive village of Lamphey. Here we dismiss our driver, and, turning across park-like meadows where cattle are grazing under the broad-limbed oaks, we soon descry the ivy-mantled ruins of Lamphey Palace.

The graceful character of the architecture, and calm, reposeful situation in this peaceful dell, combine to enhance the peculiar charm that hangs around these venerable ruins. Thanks to the timely care of their present owner, the remaining portions have been preserved from further desecration, and are freely shown to visitors who pass this way.

At Lamphey the Bishops of St. Davids possessed an episcopal manor, and built themselves a palace there; so that, from the middle of the thirteenth century, they paid frequent visits to the place. Withdrawing hither from affairs of State, they assumed the *rôle* of the paternal country squire; tilling the fat acres spread around their walls, and stocking their snug granaries, such as may still be traced at the farmstead called Lamphey Park.

John Leland, travelling this way in his tour through South Wales, tells how he 'came by meane Hills and Dales to Llanfeith, where the Bishop of St. Davids hath a place of Stoone, after Castel Fascion.'

Strolling through a ripe old garden, set round with sheltering walls, we proceed to trace such features of the fine old fabric as the hand of Time has spared to us. Passing the refectory, a picturesque building draped in ivy and Virginia-creeper, we are confronted by the tall mass

AT
LAMPHEY
PALACE.

H. J. Jimonby

of the banqueting-hall, with its pointed windows and pretty projecting chimney.

Hence a winding stair in the thickness of the wall leads to the ruined parapet. Near the east end of the hall stands the chapel, roofless now, and wreathed in luxuriant ivy; one graceful traceried window alone bearing witness to Bishop Vaughan's artistic genius.

Farther away across a verdant meadow, and standing, so to speak, *en échelon* to the main fabric, rise the ruins of the domestic apartments; approached by a dilapidated flight of outside steps, and crowned with an elegant open arcade such as is usually associated with the work of that famous builder, Bishop Gower. In a corner of the adjacent field we observe the vivarium, or fish-pond of the priory.

We now return to the neighbouring gardens, in order to sketch the picturesque little tower which stands isolated amidst trim walks and old-fashioned flower-beds.

It is difficult to assign a *raison d'être* for the existence of this quaint old structure. By some folks it has been called the gate-tower to the inner ward; but others, again, have styled it the priests' dwelling-place; and our investigations seem to point to some such use as the latter.

A stone stairway, hollowed in the thickness of the wall, leads to an upper chamber, which contains a niche (suggestive of a piscina), a fire-place, and several small windows. The peaked roof, which is modern, is surrounded by open, pointed arches corbelled out from the wall below, and finished with plain battlements. Thus, with its picturesque medley of weather-stained brick, stone and timber, touched here and there with green moss and golden lichens, this curious tower proves an attractive bit for the sketch-book.

At Lamphey Palace Robert Devereux, the ill-fated Earl of Essex, spent several years of his youth; and is reputed to have quitted the place ' the most finished gentleman of his time.'

Superstitious folk, when approaching these ruins after nightfall, while ' the moping owl doth to the moon complain,' may (or may not) have their nerves agreeably thrilled by the apparition of a mysterious white

6

lady, presumably a Devereux, who is said to haunt these historic shades at that witching hour !

Lamphey Church, which lies a short half-mile away, has been too much modernized to detain us long. The tall, plain tower has been

THE CHANCEL
HODGESTON CHURCH

preserved, however, in its original simplicity; and the large square font, of early type, has a little ornamentation of good character.

Crossing the railway bridge past *the* shop of the village, with its alluring display of miscellaneous *olla podrida* in the window, we pursue our shadows along a dusty country road; cutting off a circuitous corner by taking to a pleasant fieldpath. A bright little country maid pioneers us hence into Hodgeston, a sleepy hamlet consisting of some half-dozen whitewashed cottages clustering around the sorry remnants of a village green, now shrunk to half its old proportions owing to recent encroachments.

Obtaining the key at one of these cottages, we now make straight for the parish church, which rises beyond a grove of trees, less than a bowshot away.

Seen from the outside, this little edifice looks unostentatious enough, with its slender western tower, chancel, and nave devoid of the usual excrescences; but upon entering we soon find matter to arouse our keenest interest.

The nave is simple, though well proportioned; setting off to fullest advantage the rich and elaborate features that adorn the Decorated chancel. Good traceried windows rise upon either hand, surmounted by an open timber roof, with the pretty ball-flower ornament running around the top of the wall.

Upon the south side of the chancel stands a handsome triple sedilia; its shapely, richly-moulded arches aflame with elaborate crockets, which cluster upwards to the large, florid finials. A plain stone bench flanks the lower part of the wall, whence projects a flight of steps that gave access to the vanished rood-loft.

We also notice a dainty piscina sunk in the thickness of the wall, having a beautiful ornamental canopy, closely resembling that of the sedilia, and a fine old Norman font. One cannot but feel surprise that such rich design and delicate workmanship should be thus hidden away in this remote locality; and can only hazard the conjecture that the influence of Bishop Gower (whose handiwork is seen to such advantage in his great palace at St. Davids) must have made itself felt even in outlying parishes such as this. There is reason to suppose, too, that a religious house existed at Hodgeston in olden times, which would probably exert a refining influence upon the local craftsmen, for the monks of old were often goodly builders.

These charming features, then, provide attractive matter for the sketch-book, which keeps us pegging away until well on towards sun-down: so that, as we wend our way back to Lamphey Station, we lounge over a stile formed from some broken ship's timbers to enjoy the exquisite after-glow, which lingers still above the falling dusk as the train carries us homeward to Tenby.

ANCIENT QUERN OR HAND MILL.

CHAPTER III.

MANORBERE CASTLE: AND GIRALDUS CAMBRENSIS.

THROUGH THE courtesy of a hospitable friend, we now shift our moorings from Tenby's tourist-haunted streets, to the quiet precincts of Manorbere Castle. Within those time-honoured walls the charm of modern hospitality is enhanced by contrast with its mediæval background.

KEYS OF MANOR BERE CASTLE

Quitting the train at the little wayside station, a quarter of an hour's pleasant drive through deep lanes fringed with hartstongue fern, and gay with 'floureis white and blewe, yellow and rede,' gives us our first glimpse of the stately old pile. Crowning a low, isolated hill, the castle stands out 'four square to all the winds of heaven' against a silvery expanse of the distant ocean; for, as old Leland says: 'This place is not in the Hyeway, but standith neere the shore of the Severn Se.'

A country lad opens a gate giving access to a rough meadow, flanked by the remains of barbican walls and ruined bastions; traversing which we presently draw rein before the broad, landward front of the castle. Crossing the grim but inoffensive drawbridge, our friend explains the ingenious device by which, in the 'good old times,' an intruder must perforce 'turn turtle' upon a sort of human beetle-trap. Overhead are seen the openings whence the garrison might pour down 'something lingering and humorous, with molten lead in it,' by way of warm welcome to the foe.

Passing beneath the ivy-mantled gate-tower, we emerge upon the spacious greensward of the inner court, which is enclosed on every hand by hoary walls and turrets, whose weather-beaten ruins tell of heavy treatment at the hand of Father Time.

For it is a notable fact in the history of Manorbere Castle, and one to which we are indebted for its relative state of preservation, that, unlike its great neighbours of Pembroke and Carew, it has never withstood a siege. Moreover, having ceased to be inhabited at a very early period, this castle has preserved unaltered the salient features of its construction. The architecture is very simple and massive, being indeed almost entirely devoid of ornament. Some of the apartments retain the plain, pointed stone vault, devoid of ribs, so frequently met

MANORBERE CASTLE.
FROM THE EAST.

with in South Wallian castles; while several of those circular chimneys, peculiar to the locality, rise above the crumbling battlements.

Continuing our stroll around the inner court we observe, hard by the great gateway, the warders' room, with its narrow window commanding the entrance. Behind it rises the huge, circular 'Bull' Tower; a massive structure honeycombed with quaint little chambers approached by a winding stone stair, and connected with the gate-tower by a narrow passage in the thickness of the walls. Along the eastern side of the court extends a long range of apartments, which constitute the modern residence. These were resuscitated by Mr. J. R. Cobb, a

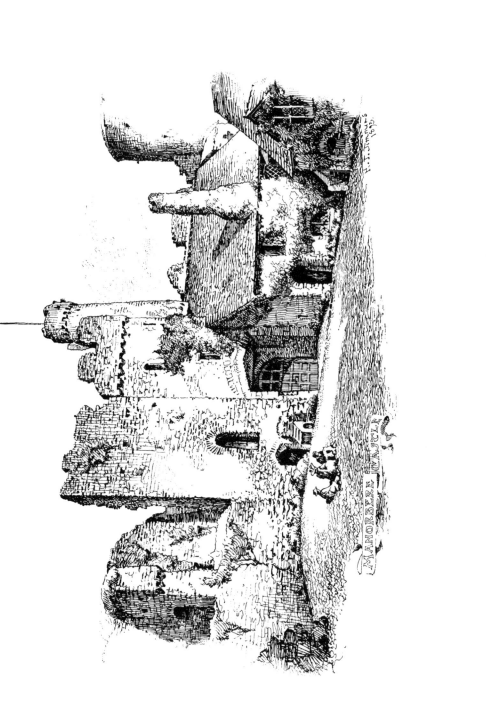

MANORBEER CASTLE

former occupant, who restored the castle in so admirable and conscien-
tious a manner, that the modern additions in no wise detract from their
venerable surroundings. Farther away in the same direction lie the
ruined kitchens, with their huge projecting chimneys, and ovens of such

MANORBERE CASTLE

capacity that, as tradition avers, the lord of the domain was wont to
regale his guests upon oxen roasted whole !

Traversing the sunny castle-garth, we pass a circular receptacle
formed in the ground for melting the lead aforesaid. Close at hand is
a deep draw-well, half full of water. Some twenty feet down this well
is a blocked-up archway which was opened years ago by old 'Billy,'

7

the local factotum, who discovered dark, subterranean passages running hence beneath the adjacent ruins. Here he stumbled against casks and kegs left behind by the smuggler folk, who in former days carried on their illicit traffic around the neighbouring coast. At the same time, as a 'blind' for the Excise officers, they carried on a traffic in grain, which was stored for the purpose in large barns outside the castle.

At the farther end of the courtyard rise the picturesque walls and arches of a lofty group of buildings, containing the banqueting-hall and chapel. This appears to have been the handsomest part of the castle; and the great hall, with its broad flight of stone steps and stately range of pointed windows overlooking the sea, must indeed have been a noble apartment. Beneath it, in grim contrast, lurks a series of dark, windowless dungeons.

Entering the chapel by a flight of ruinous steps fringed with sprays of spleenwort fern, we explore its dimly-lighted recesses, and discern traces of half obliterated colour decoration. Clambering by a narrow stone stairway to the grass-grown roof, we awaken the resentful clamour of a colony of jackdaws; anon we peer into the tiny chamber for the priest, and dive into the gloomy crypt, with its low-vaulted roof and fireplace improvised from a desecrated tomb.

Then out once more into the castle garth, to follow the loopholed wall. This terminates in the many-sided Pembroke Tower, which, bowered in climbing plants, boasts a certain diminutive chamber wherein, as the local tradition runs, Giraldus Cambrensis, the famous Welsh historian, was born. Thence ensues another stretch of lofty wall, backed by a series of curious flying buttresses: and our peregrination is completed beneath the hoary, lichen-clad stonework of the great tower beside the entrance gateway. This is the oldest part of the castle, and (with apologies to the local tradition) probably the only portion of it that dates as far back as the days of the worthy Giraldus.

The water-gate, set deep in the seaward wall, is flanked by a huge mass of stonework which still bears traces of the smugglers' ineffectual efforts to dislodge it. Following a rough track that winds down the rocky slope, we stroll onward beside a pretty rill of water meandering,

MANORBEER · CASTLE ·

amidst bullrushes and marsh marigolds, to the moss-grown wheel of the castle mill. Here we linger upon the rustic footbridge to enjoy a charming retrospect. The gray walls of the grim old castle, crowning the low, steep hill we have just descended, are reflected in the placid stream at our feet. A group of low-roofed cottages, and the mill with its plashing wheel, nestle in the valley beneath; while the towers and gables of the quaint old parish church peep from a rival hill that fronts the sea.

The western flank of the castle looks down upon a weed-grown marsh, occupying the site of a lake that formerly protected it upon that side. Beside the marsh stands a picturesque old stone pigeon-house, smothered in ivy and golden lichens; beyond which extends a secluded vale shaded by oak, ash and holly, that formed part of the ancient park or chase of Manorbere. The whole scene has a quiet beauty of its own very pleasant to contemplate.

Meanwhile, after tackling this fascinating bit, we roam across the wind-blown sandhills, where a derelict boat, lying high and dry above high-water mark, offers a convenient resting-place for the noontide *siesta*. Stretching our limbs upon the warm, dry sand, and gazing dreamily across the deep-blue line of the bay, we call to mind a certain glowing description of the Manorbere of seven long centuries ago. Gerald de Barri, the author of this panegyric (better known as Giraldus Cambrensis), can scarce find words to express his admiration for the home of his boyhood.

' The castle called Maenor Pyrr,' says Gerald, ' is excellently defended by towers and outworks, and is situated on the summit of a hill extending on the western side towards the seaport; having on the northern and southern sides a fine fish-pond under the walls, as conspicuous for its grand appearance as for the depth of its water; and a beautiful orchard on the same side enclosed on one part by a vineyard, and on the other by a wood remarkable for the projection of its rocks and the height of its hazel-trees. To the right of the promontory, between the castle and the church, near the site of a very large lake and mill, a rivulet of never-failing water flows through a valley rendered sandy by the violence of the winds.'

The same enthusiastic writer also portrays for us the main features of the circumjacent country: ' Towards the west the Severn Sea, bending its course to Ireland, enters a hollow bay at some distance from the castle; and the southern rocks, if more extended towards the north, would render it an admirable harbour for shipping. From this point you may see almost all the ships from greater Britain, which the east wind drives towards Ireland. The land is well supplied with corn, sea-fish and wines, purchased abroad; and—what is of more importance—from its neighbourhood to Ireland it enjoys a mild climate.

' Dimetia therefore, with its seven *cantrefs*, is the most beautiful, as well as the most powerful district in Wales; Pembroch the finest part of the province of Dimetia; and the place I have just described the most beautiful part of Pembroch. It is evident, therefore, that Maenor Pyrr is the Paradise of all Wales !'

Born at Manorbere Castle in the year 1146, Gerald de Barri was the youngest son of William de Barri, Lord of Manorbere; grandson of Gerald de Windsor, Governor of Pembroke Castle; and nephew of David Fitz-Gerald, Bishop of St. Davids, from whom he received his early education; while upon the maternal side Gerald was descended from Rhys ap Tydwr, one of the princes of Wales. The career of one thus born, so to speak, in the purple, was from the outset pretty well assured. Thus we find the worthy Gerald promoted from the living of Tenby to a fat canonry at Hereford Cathedral; and presently the snug archdeaconry of St. Davids falls to his lot.

About this time, Gerald joined with Archbishop Baldwin to preach the Crusade throughout South Wales; when he kept a diary of his proceedings which has proved of no little entertainment to after-comers.

During his long and eventful career Gerald de Barri paid three several visits to Rome, in order to push his interests at headquarters. He accompanied Henry II. to France, and was entrusted by that monarch with the education of his promising son John, of Magna Charta fame. Upon the death of his uncle the Bishop, Gerald made strenuous efforts to obtain the coveted appointment of his native see, refusing all other preferments ; but, failing of success, he retired in dudgeon from active life, and spent the rest of his days in writing those literary ' remains ' that have afforded so much interest to antiquaries.

Gerald de Barri appears to have been a man of studious temperament. He became, as Lambarde quaintly puts it, ' wel learned and, as tyme served, eloquent.' He was, moreover, a great writer, and being much given to disputation, called together the literary *élite* of Oxford and read his own works to them. He next proceeded to feast his

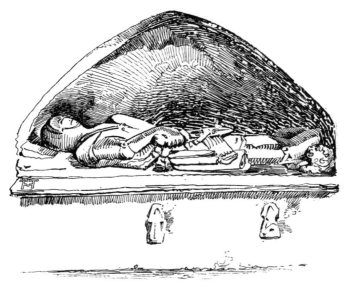

DE BARRI TOMB, MANORBERE.

learned critics into a satisfactory state of good humour with things in general, and his own literary effusions in particular ; an event which he himself describes as ' a magnificent affair, a return of the Golden Age, an unparalleled event, in England at all events.'

In person Gerald is portrayed as remarkably tall, his face being strongly marked by large, shaggy eyebrows ; and it has been well said that, in spite of certain undeniable defects of character, he was probably inspired with a genuine love for the land of his birth, and a desire to upraise therein an independent Kymric Church owning allegiance to the Bishop of St. Davids as its spiritual head.

Gerald de Barri was gathered to his fathers, at a ripe old age, in the year 1220. He is reputed to have been buried in St. Davids Cathedral; where *at least one* tomb is pointed out as the last resting-place of this great ecclesiastic.

Little is recorded of the subsequent history of Manorbere Castle. The place appears to have been abandoned at an early period; its hanging woods and vineyards were abandoned to decay, whilst its dismantled walls and subterranean vaults harboured bands of lawless freebooters, who haunted these coasts a century ago. Wild work went forward at Manorbere in those half-forgotten days. It is related how a certain famous smuggler, notorious for his desperate enterprises, eluded the vigilance of the revenue men by running his vessel ashore near the headland ycleped the Priest's Nose; and conveying his illicit cargo, under cover of night, to the cellars with which the neighbourhood abounded.

Rousing ourselves at length from these cogitations on the sand-hills, we put the best foot foremost and hie away past a spring of pure water known as the Druid's Well, to the sunny slopes of that selfsame Priest's Nose. Scrambling warily amidst brakes of prickly furze, we presently espy a mighty cromlech standing in a nook of the hill, beside the narrow path. A soft westerly breeze draws in 'gently, very gently from the sea,' as we perch beside this relic of the immemorial past; wafting the scent of wild thyme and gorse over warm, crisp turf that shimmers beneath the lusty summer sunshine. Hence unfolds yet another charming view of the gray old castle, set amidst a breadth of feathery woodland that clusters under the lee of the sheltering hill. A turn of the head reveals the varied line of coast stretching away, league upon league, past the groves of Stackpole to the bluff, perpendicular landfall of St. Govan's Head.

Returning to quarters by another route we fetch a wide compass round; pursuing the path that hugs the shore, which, hereabouts, is indented by several fissures of very peculiar character. A short distance beyond the cromlech we encounter the first of these; a chasm so narrow that a boy might leap across it, yet of imposing depth, with sides as smooth and perpendicular as any house wall, and floored with the seething ocean.

A quarter of a mile farther on we strike a little way inland, to investigate a still more remarkable *lusus naturæ* of a similar kind.

The Church Path ~
Manorbere

Here the insidious onslaught of the waves has tunnelled beneath the intervening cliff, and penetrated far into the land; excavating a dark, narrow, and profound fissure in the perpendicular strata of the Old Red sandstone; so that, gazing seaward through the cleft, we can see the foaming surf sparkling in the sunlight upon the rocks beyond. Thence we extend our ramble to Castle Head, a rocky point jutting boldly out to sea, and scarped with the broad, fern-clad furrows of a prehistoric earthwork. This appears to have been the stronghold of some invader from over seas; for the protecting banks curve inland, and, sweeping down to the rocks on either hand, enclose the outer extremity of the headland. Secured thus against attack upon their landward flank, the occupants were protected in rear by the broad expanse of the 'inviolate ocean,' whose restless billows, surging far below, mingle their music in wild harmony with the harsh cries of countless sea-fowl.

8

Breasting the rough ascent, we now march across the upland meadows of Parson's Piece; making in a 'bee-line' for Manorbere Church, whose slim gray tower peers over an intervening bank. Perched high aloft upon a bleak hillside, across whose treeless heights 'breathes the shrill spirit of the western wind,' this venerable fabric rises in lonely isolation, and confronts in peaceful rivalry the towers and battlements of the grim old fortalice that crowns the opposite hill.

For quaint picturesqueness, and the singular grouping of its various parts, this curious old church stands unrivalled, even in this land of remarkable churches, combining as it does almost every feature character-istic of such buildings throughout the locality. Originally in all proba-bility a cruciform structure, the church has apparently been added to at various times in a capricious fashion; so that the exterior now presents the quaintest imaginable variety of walls, windows and gables; all jumbled together in seemingly haphazard fashion, and falling into fantastic groups, as may be seen from the adjoining sketch.

It will be noticed that one of the gables is surmounted by the original bell-cot, which probably existed prior to the erection of the tower; the latter rises above a medley of roofs upon the northern side of the chancel, and contains a bell inscribed with the legend: EXALTEMUS NOMEN DOMINI, 1639.

Passing around to the south porch, we enter a low nave arched over with a slightly-pointed, stone-vaulted ceiling. Strange, low, rudely-fashioned arches, entirely disdaining the support of pillars, rise sheer from the level of the floor upon either hand, giving access to the narrow aisles behind. These arches are, unfortunately, so enveloped in the general coating of whitewash, that it is impossible now to discover whether they were originally built as arches, proper, or are merely open-ings cut through the walls when the aisles were added to the nave. A little window of early type opens above one of these arches; the sole survivor of some old windows that existed previous to the building of the aisles.

Short, tunnel-like transepts open out on either hand, the one towards the north having a low ceiling, crossed by the curious arched

MANORBERE
CHVRCH.

ribs seen in our sketch above. The gangway that formerly gave access to the rood-loft now leads, in a queer, tortuous course, from the north aisle across the adjacent transept to the tower, which is entered by a door high aloft in the wall.

To the right a 'squint' passage opens skew-wise into the chancel, where, beneath a plain arched recess, lies the recumbent stone effigy of a Crusader clad in chain mail, having his legs crossed at the knees and sword and shield, charged with the arms of De Barri, beside him. This monument commemorates one of the ancient lords of Manor-bere, who 'came over with the Conqueror,' and shared with Fitz-Hamon and his knights in the partition of these lands.

The handsome traceried screen that stretches athwart the narrow chancel arch was erected about five-and-twenty years ago, when a vigorous effort was made to arrest the deplorable condition of ruin and decay, to which time and neglect had reduced this interesting church.

A few ivy-mantled fragments of an ancient structure that formerly served as the parish school, are supposed to be the remains of a chantry founded by the De Barri who lies buried in the church.

We now stroll leisurely homeward through the gloaming, while the slender young moon peers over the shoulder of a neighbouring hill. As we approach the castle, its shadowy front looms darkly silhouetted upon a daffodil and emerald sky ; while the zenith is still suffused with translucent rosy light, and the pale stars peep one by one as the day-light slowly wanes. Now the little flittermice awake once more to life, and flicker to and fro with wavering flight ; while a colony of chatter-ing jackdaws discusses the day's events upon the ruined battlements. Yonder, like a thief of the night, a great white owl steals silently by, soft as a drift of thistledown, yet keen as fate to 'spot' the errant mouse, roaming in search of a meal too far from home.

Thus we recross the drawbridge to the hospitable abode, whose latticed windows emit a heartsome ray of light that seems a lode-star to the wayfarers. Pretty tired after our long day's ramble, we clamber up the corkscrew stair to a certain turret chamber, where, in next to no time, we lose ourselves in the drowsy arms of Morpheus.

The busy man, hard pressed by the *Sturm und Drang* of city life, may find at Manorbere recreation in the truest sense; and should he be blessed with a congenial hobby, he may entertain himself in this secluded spot to his heart's content.

To the lover of Nature the place offers many attractions. In the course of rambles around the varied coastline, or amidst the hills and dales of the inland country, the wanderer with a turn that way may study the mellow lichen-clad rocks of the Old Red sandstone; and will not fail to notice their well-defined junction at Skrinkle Haven with the limestone formation, which reappears across the Sound in the cave-worn crags of Caldey. Or, again, he may note how the salmon-red ploughlands of the Ridgeway attest the presence of the older rocks, as they rise from the superincumbent stratum of the mountain limestone.

These conditions afford, within a limited compass, a great diversity of soil and situation; providing a congenial habitat to many varieties of ferns and wild-flowers. The botanist will look for prizes amongst the rich pastures of the Vale of St. Florence, the woodland paths around St. Issells, and the lush marshlands of Penally; while the sandy burrows of Tenby, Lydstep and Castle Martin, and even the crumbling ruins of some castle or ancient priory, will yield their tale of treasure for the vasculum.

Indeed, wander whither he may, the lover of Nature will find a wealth of beauty on every hand. Let him clamber amidst the tumbled boulders, where the samphire thrives on the salt sea spray; and explore the rock-pools left by the receding tide, whose weed-fringed depths are tenanted by plump sea-urchins, nestling sociably among zoophytes, sponges, and delicate 'lady's-fingers.' Or he may choose to wander along the sands of Saundersfoot and Tenby, where haply he may light upon rare shells of many a dainty hue; while queer little crabs scuttle hither and thither amidst the stranded starfish, and other derelict flotsam and jetsam left behind by the receding tide.

And as the changing seasons cast their ever-varying charm upon land and sea, the artist in search of 'fresh woods and pastures new' will find, in this unfrequented country, endless subjects ready to his hand worthy the brush of a Brett, or an Alfred Parsons. Perchance he will set up his easel where the ruddy sandstone cliffs, soaring in weather-stained crags above broad sweeps of untrodden sand, are crowned with a diadem of golden gorse; while a breadth of sunlit sea stretching away to the horizon will serve as an excellent background. Or haply he may plant his white umbrella in some secluded nook, where a picturesque old cottage, with mighty, bulging chimney and moss-grown roofs, nestles beneath a group of wind-swept ash trees; the softly folding landscape lines showing faintly beyond.

Many a beauty-spot such as this gladdens the wayfarer as he roams through the by-ways of this pleasant land; and the landscape-painter may easily 'go farther and fare worse,' than by spending a season in Pembrokeshire.

CHAPTER IV.

PEMBROKE TOWN AND CASTLE. STACKPOLE AND THE SOUTHERN
COAST.

IN COURSE of time the *Wanderlust* returns in full force upon us; so bidding farewell to our hospitable entertainers, we transfer ourselves bag and baggage to the county-town; in order to explore from that convenient starting-point the remoter recess of South Pembrokeshire.

The district locally known as the Stackpole Country forms part of the hundred of Castle Martin, and is the southernmost land of the county. Lying apart from any town or railway, it is somewhat difficult of access; but though boasting few striking features to attract the ordinary tourist, it yet offers no small attractions to the wanderer who can appreciate 'the pleasures of the quiet eye.'

Threading our way at first amidst rather intricate lanes, we pass once more through Hodgeston village, whence our route is all plain sailing. Near Lamphey Church we fall into the main road, which runs in a bee-line beside softly-swelling hills, until the long street of Pembroke is entered at its eastern end.

The 'lie' of this town has been not inaptly likened to the shape of a herring-bone; the castle precincts occupying the head (whereof the great donjon answers to the eye), while the long main street, with its branching lanes and gardens, suggests the vertebral bone of the fish with its radial spines. *Apropos* of the situation of the town, we refer to our trusty Leland and read that 'Pembroch standith upon an arme of Milforde, the which, about a mile beyond the Towne, creketh in so that it almost peninsulateth the Towne, that standith on a veri main Rokki ground. The Towne is well waullid and hath iii gates by Est, West and North; of which the Est gate is fairest and strongest, having afore it a compasid Tour not rofid in; the entering whereof is a Port colys, *ex solide ferro.*'

PEMBROKE.

Neither gate nor 'compasid Tour' now spans the prosaic-looking street; and the houses in this eastern suburb have small pretensions to beauty. We catch a hasty glimpse, however, of the 'two paroche chirches' discovered by our author; and entertain ourselves *en route* by trying to pronounce the curious, unfamiliar surnames such as Hopla, Treweeks, Malefant and Tyzard, emblazoned above the shop-fronts; while an occasional Godolphin, Pomeroy or Harcourt, attests the strain of sang-azure that lingers yet among the *bourgeoisie* of the ancient borough.

Midway adown the High Street rises a mighty elm, whose spreading branches quite overshadow the adjacent dwellings. Presently we catch a glimpse of Pembroke Castle, beyond a pretty vista of old-fashioned structures whose quaint, irregular outlines stand sharply cut against the clear sky.

The records of this great historic fortress would alone suffice to fill a bulky volume; the best account of the earls, earldom and castle of Pembroke being, perhaps, that by G. T. Clark, Esq.; and there is a detailed description of the building by the present proprietor, J. R. Cobb, Esq. We will not attempt, therefore, to give more than a slight outline of its past history.

Pembroke Castle was originally built by Arnulph de Montgomery, in the reign of William Rufus; and it was greatly enlarged and strengthened by Earl Strongbow, the invader of Ireland, who held it in the time of Henry I.

A romantic story is related of his predecessor, the King's castellan, Gerald de Windsor, who espoused the beautiful but notorious Nesta. A certain Welsh chieftain, named Owen ap Cadwgan, beheld the famous beauty presiding one day with her ladies at a tournament (like the moon amidst her satellites); when, sighing like Alcestis for the Queen of night, the enamoured warrior determined to possess himself of his seductive charmer. Obtaining access to the castle at dead of night, Owen wrested his victim from the arms of her outraged lord, and carried her off to his stronghold among the mountains. Though a large reward was offered by the King to anyone who should capture or slay the outlawed man, it was eight long years before justice was vindicated, when Gerald, meeting his adversary, put an end to his career by an avenging arrow.

But to return to history. William, Earl Mareschal of Pembroke, was honoured with a visit from that sorry monarch, King John. During the Edwardian period, the castle was enlarged and strengthened by the addition of the outer ward. In 1457 Henry Tudor, Earl of

PEMBROKE CASTLE

Richmond (afterwards King Henry VII.), was born at Pembroke Castle.

During the Civil Wars the garrison made a gallant defence against a large force under Oliver Cromwell. One tragic episode that closed the eventful days of the siege may be mentioned here. Upon the fall of the castle the three leaders, Poyer, Mayor of the town, Powell, Governor of the castle, and Laugharne, the whilom Parliamentary Colonel, were expressly exempted from the pardon extended to the garrison. These three men were condemned to death : but Parliament in its clemency resolving to punish only one of them, they were directed by Cromwell's orders to draw lots as to who should suffer the penalty. Two papers were inscribed ' Life given by God '; the third was a blank. A child drew the lots, when the blank fell to the ill-fated Poyer ; who was afterwards shot in the Piazza, Covent Garden, 'dying very penitently,' as we are told. After the fortress was delivered into Cromwell's hands, it was so effectually dismantled that, to this day, the results of his destructive work are only too manifest.

The ruins of Pembroke Castle still present, after the lapse of centuries of neglect and decay, a truly magnificent appearance. The massive towers and ivy-curtained walls crown a bold and rocky eminence, that rises abruptly from the tidal waters of Milford Haven ; sweeping around the landward face of the promontory, and enclosing a broad and spacious castle garth.

In the centre rises the great donjon tower, which stands as an enduring memorial of William de la Grace, the great Earl Mareschal, who in all probability designed the main fabric of the castle as we see it to-day. An imposing *coup d'œil* of the ruins may be obtained by turning down Dark Lane, crossing the old bridge that spans the stream hard beneath the castle, and entering a timber-yard close by. Prominent in the view is a lofty tower, mantled in glossy-green ivy and pierced with graceful pointed windows, that soars from the river brink, enclosing, deep below its foundations, that ' mervelous vault called the Hogan,' whence the garrison in olden times drew their supplies of water.

Beside the tower extends a long stretch of ivy-clad wall, rooted in the living rock and broken at intervals by shapely turrets; over which peep the upper works of the central keep. The spars and cordage of some stranded coasting vessels, and a group of men calking their weather-beaten timbers, lend an added charm to an exceedingly picturesque scene.

We are indebted to Leland for the ensuing description of the castle as it appeared in the days of bluff King Hal: 'The Castel stondeth hard by the waul on a hard Rokke, and is veri large and stronge, being doble wardid. In the atter ward I saw the chaumbre wher King Henri the vii was borne; in knowledge whereof a chymmeney is now made, with the armes and Badges of King Henri vii. In the botom of the great stronge Towr, in the inner warde, is a mervelous vault called the Hogan.' Another chronicler of very different stamp, the late Professor Freeman, thus records his impressions of this interesting pile: 'Pembroke Castle remarkably combines elevation and massiveness, so that its effect is one of vast general bulk. It is another conspicuous instance of the majesty often accruing to dismantled buildings, which they could never have possessed when in a perfect state.'

Traversing the outer barbican that protected the deep-set entrance, we pause to marvel at the elaborate defences of double portcullis and thick, nail-studded doors, commanded by loopholed guard-chambers, set within the gloomy arches of the gate-tower. The latter presents a stately front, flanked by attached round towers, overlooking the inner court; and contains a number of fine apartments for the accommodation of distinguished guests.

We next turn our attention to the adjacent barbican tower, whose massive walls are seamed from top to base by huge, gaping rents, through which the daylight peers; yet so great is their tenacity they still remain intact, and support the original stone roof. Each story is pierced with loopholes, ingeniously constructed to prevent missiles entering from below. The spacious courtyard enclosed by the outer walls is carpeted with velvety turf, whereon 'the quality' are wont to foregather from far and near to wield the tennis-racket, and contest for 'deuce' and 'love' upon the selfsame spot where, in the brave days of old, the Harcourts and De Valances, and all the flower of Norman chivalry, flung down the gauntlet or broke a lance upon the field of honour, while fair spectators waved encouragement from every arch and balcony.

Beside the great central keep a labyrinth of crumbling walls, towers and arches, mainly of Edwardian date, cluster together in 'most admired confusion.' Here are pointed out the remains of the chapel of St. Nicholas, given by Montgomery to the Norman abbey of Sayes. A chamber is usually pointed out, in the building called the Exchequer, as that in which Henry VII. first saw the light; but Mr. Cobb suggests a room in the tower overlooking Westgate Hill. Unfortunately, the arms and badges noticed by Leland no longer exist to mark the scene of that interesting event.

Clambering down a flight of broken steps in an obscure corner of the North Hall, we enter the vast cavern known as the Wogan; a very curious and characteristic feature of Pembroke Castle. As we ramble over the damp and slippery floor, by such light as can struggle in through the huge sally-port and a narrow, pointed window, we find ourselves in a spacious, natural vault sunk deep in the living rock; its rugged walls and roof festooned with hartstongue fern, and stained by oozing moisture—a weird, fantastic spot, such as the shade of the primæval cave-dweller might frequent, should he elect to revisit the glimpses of the moon.

Sheer from the 'main Rokke' upon which the castle is founded, rises the vast, circular keep or donjon tower, which formed the central stronghold of the fortress. This is undoubtedly one of the most ancient parts of the castle, having been erected by William Strongbow the elder, 'Rector Regis et Regni,' as he proudly styled himself; who was Earl Mareschal of Pembroke during the reigns of Richard Cœur-de-Lion and John.

This imposing structure impresses every beholder by the vast proportions and stern simplicity of its mighty bulk. The massive walls rise to a height of more than 75 feet, and are of amazing thickness and solidity; a spiral staircase, set deep within the wall, gave access to the several floors and to the rampart around the summit, which commands a wide sweep of the circumjacent landscape, with a glimpse of the winding Haven. The floors have long since fallen away, though the holes for the beams that supported them may still be seen, and two huge fireplaces with yawning archways of enormous size. Lancet-windows and loops for the archers open out here and there; one of the former, high up the wall (which appears in our sketch), retaining some touches of ornamentation.

'The Toppe of this round Towr,' as Leland quaintly puts it, 'is gatherid with a Rose of Stone;' and, despite seven centuries of rough weather and hard usage, the huge fabric appears intrinsically little the worse for wear, and capable still of making a stand ''gainst the tooth of time and razure of oblivion,' for many a long year to come.

A stroll around the outer walls, and a peep at the Monkton Tower, completes our perambulation of Pembroke Castle. With its neighbours of Manorbere, Tenby and Carew, Pembroke formed a quadrilateral, planted to guard this exposed district against attack from without: moreover, as Professor Freeman has pointed out, this time-honoured fortress has a special interest for the antiquarian student, as affording an unusually complete example of a mediæval castle protecting a civic settlement.

In the course of a ramble around the town, we turn into old St. Mary's Church, a handsome edifice containing some curiously sculptured tombs and a brand-new reredos. A low, massive tower rises at one end of the church; and hard by it stands the quaint cupola of the old market-house, which, adorned with a clock, and little figures of boys by way of pinnacles, makes a pretty show in the view along the High Street. Many of the older houses have an unpretentious charm about them, with their antiquated bow-windows and wide oak staircases with twisted balusters. Not a few of the better sort have old-fashioned gardens to the rear, abloom in summer days with homely flowers, and redolent of honeysuckle, lavender and jasmine.

Of the three town gates described by Leland, a scanty remnant of the West Gate is all that now survives. Proceeding down the main street, with the castle walls upon our right hand, we pass a group of cottages jumbled all together upon a rising bank beside the highway, whence they are approached by flights of crazy steps. A glance at our sketch of these picturesque old structures (which have already been partially 'restored' since this view was taken) will show the broken arch of the demolished West Gate, and the castle walls frowning across the roadway, which has been widened out since the gate was removed.

THE OLD WEST GATE,
PEMBROKE.

At the bottom of the hill we skirt the salt waters of a creek, or 'pill,' to use the local term, that 'gulfith in' beneath the shaggy bank upon which the castle stands. Traversing the bridge, we mount up-wards again, and turn aside into a hollow way where a cluster of thatched cottages, half hidden beneath embowering woodbine, stands high above the roadway ; whence time-worn steps clamber to their lowly porches.

But, *vis-à-vis* across the lane, rises a building whose unfamiliar aspect at once arrests our attention. This is Monkton Old Hall, whose massive front of dark-hued stone is pierced with narrow windows, set beneath a low browed archway.   Upon passing to the rear we stumble upon a real old-world nook, where a crazy old ' Flemish ' chimney rears above a curious medley of weather-stained roofs and gables.

With the courteous assent of the proprietor, we now take a glance round the interior.   Passing through a low, pointed doorway, we thread our way amidst tortuous passages, and enter a lofty apartment.

The Priors Dwelling
Monkton.

A large stone arch in the wall at one end encloses two quaint little slits of windows (or peepholes, rather), with a similar opening lower down, overlooking the approach from the outer entrance.   A tortuous stairway gives access to the upper regions, which contain various small chambers, one of them having a fine old stone chimney-piece.

But the most notable feature of the place is a large, oblong chamber cut out of the rock, with vaulted roof of Norman date supported by massive ribs, which occupies the lower part of the house.   It has a separate entrance from the road, and a big fireplace opening to the circular chimney - shaft above mentioned.

Monkton Priory, of which this old hall appears to have been the hospitium, or Prior's dwelling, was founded in 1098 ; and was subordinate to St. Martin's Abbey at Séez, in Normandy.

Resuming our ramble, we turn through a wicket at the top of the road, and follow a narrow path that leads to the great south porch of

Monkton Priory Church. The venerable edifice has a picturesque appearance; with the ruined walls and traceried windows of an ancient chapel beside the chancel, and the Norman porch breaking the line of the nave roof. Upon passing around to the north side, we are struck by the archaic simplicity of the long, Norman nave, strengthened with vast rugged buttresses and lighted by narrow, round-arched windows, set few and far between. The chapel above mentioned projects upon this side; and the ground is broken by traces of buildings that formed part of the precincts of the ancient priory.

The lonely dwelling to the westward was until lately used as the rectory house; an unpretending edifice, whose weather-stained coating of rough-cast partially conceals rows of old corbels, and other half-obliterated features. Looking hence across Monkton Pill we have a fine view of the castle, with its picturesque array of broken towers and bastions, and a quaint old stone pigeon-cot down in the valley which formed an appendage to that lordly *ménage*. While enjoying this goodly scene, a summer shower sweeps up from the sea, and robs us for a time of the enchanting prospect; but ere long the old fortress reappears beneath a brilliant arc of rainbow, glowing in borrowed splendours under the warm rays of the declining sun.

*   *   *   *   *   *

'Night's candles are burnt out, and jocund Day
Stands tiptoe on the misty mountain-tops,'

as we fare cheerily forth, on the morrow's morn, to explore the remoter recesses of that secluded district ycleped the Stackpole Country.

Our footsteps echo loudly as we trudge through Pembroke's deserted street, where as yet a few half-awakened housemaids, and labouring men going to their day's work, are the only signs of life.

Nearing the railway-station we turn aside into a narrow, tortuous lane; cross the stream that fed the old town moat and, passing a water-mill beside a disused limestone quarry, we strike up the steady ascent of Windmill Hill; catching *en route* a glimpse of the time-worn steeple of St. Daniel's Church, now used merely as a cemetery chapel.

Upon winning the crest of the ridge the country opens out ahead, showing a cluster of tall church towers clear against the skyline; and then we drop sharply down one of those short, steep 'pinches'. that make such heavy work for the horses hereabouts.

Groups of country-folk jaunt by to market in carts of primitive build, propelled by strong, well-cared-for looking donkeys; and thus, *a poco a poco* as they say in Italy, we work our passage through quiet, unfrequented by-ways; startling a shy rabbit here and there, or flushing a buxom partridge and her brood from beneath our very feet.

Sir Elidur de Stackpole

Now and again we pause to catch the throstle's mellow song, or to watch the easy movements of a pair of sparrow-hawks, as they wheel in slow, graceful gyrations through the air.

By-and-by we come to Cheriton; a tiny hamlet with a comely church, whose tall, ivy-clad tower rises from a wooded dell. In the church-yard stands an ancient cross smothered in creepers, and the stepping-block for those who rode to church in bygone days.

In the north wall of the chancel, beneath a handsome, canopied recess of somewhat unusual character, lies the effigy of its reputed founder, Sir Elidur de Stackpole.

The figure has a grave and dignified appearance; it is clad in a suit of chain-and-plate mail, and has sword, shield and large spurs. The worthy knight is represented with crossed legs, as having fought in the wars of the Crusades; at the time, no doubt, when Baldwyn and Gerald of Manorbere were inciting the people to that famous enterprise.

The base of this monument is divided into six panels, in each of which is a figure beneath a cusped and crocketed arch. These quaint little effigies show a curious variety of costume and expression, and are worth close examination. Upon the opposite, or southern, side of the chancel is the figure of a lady, apparently of Edwardian date. The head is covered with a square hood, and is supported by two kneeling angels. This effigy is very well executed, and in an unusually good state of preservation.

In the adjacent chantry we notice the early seventeenth-century monument of ' Roger Lorte, late Lorde of the Mannor of Stackpoole.' This singular erection is enriched with the painted figures of Sir Roger, his lady, and their twelve children, and bears a pious inscription in the peculiar style of the period. Under the window of this chantry lies a disused altar stone bearing the following inscription, which we respectfully submit for antiquaries to exercise their wits upon: CAMU ORIS FILI FANNUC.

Hard beneath the church we plunge into a woodland path, and follow the meanderings of a prattling brook which hurries along, beneath the cool shade of overarching trees, to the lake-like river that skirts the broad demesne of Stackpole Court.

The variety and luxuriance of the forest trees that flourish in this sheltered locality, are all the more striking in a country where well-developed timber is, as a rule, conspicuous by its absence; for the rigorous gales that sweep across the more exposed uplands, give to the struggling vegetation that leeward slant which is a characteristic of many a Pembrokeshire landscape.

Pleasant it is, turning from the glare of the dusty roadway, to saunter beneath these leafy aisles of smooth-stemmed beech and knotty oak, mountain-ash, ilex and Scotch fir; and to push our way through intertwining thickets of bramble, wild-rose and ivy, enmeshed by the clinging woodbine and traveller's joy; while all the time the mercury, in less-favoured spots, is climbing steadily towards the eighties.

Crossing a rustic bridge that spans the lake, we pause to watch the slim, brown trout darting in every direction beneath the water-lilies that adorn its placid surface; when, suddenly, a brace of dusky waterfowl, alarmed by our intrusion, dart off with an impetuous splash and trail away in rapid flight to the shelter of the ozier-beds.

Ere long the broad, gray front of Stackpole Court comes into view beyond a stretch of velvety greensward; the massive porch being flanked

STACKPOLE.

by two small Spanish field-guns of antiquated pattern, bearing the titles 'La Destruidora' and 'La Tremenda.' The existing mansion was built by an ancestor of the present Lord Cawdor, upon the site of the baronial residence of that same Sir Elidur de Stackpole, whose tomb we have so lately seen at Cheriton.

The older house had experienced a chequered career. After weathering many troubles in mediæval times, it was garrisoned by the King's troops during the Civil Wars; when its stout old walls offered such effective resistance to the Parliamentary cannon, that they did but little execution.

Stackpole is now the residence of the noble 'Thane of Cawdor,' whose ancestor acquired the estate by marriage with Miss Lort, the sole heiress to all these broad acres.

The mansion contains some interesting works of art and relics of antiquity, including a portrait by Romney of the famous Lady Hamilton; a fine painting of Admiral Sir George Campbell, G.C.B., who captured the French invaders at Fishguard in 1797; and a curious old map of the county, adorned with shields and armorial devices.

THE HIRLAS HORN

That famous drinking-cup the 'Hirlas horn' was formerly to be seen at Stackpole, but has since been removed to Golden Grove, in Carmarthenshire. This curious treasure is mounted in silver, and is supported upon an oval plinth by two silver quadrupeds, as shown in our sketch. The latter are probably the only remaining portions of the original horn, presented by Henry of Richmond to his faithful enter-tainer, Dafydd ap Ievan, while resting at the castle of Llwyn Dafydd, in Cardiganshire, on his way to Bosworth Field.

Upon faring forth again, we are struck with admiration of the splendid groups of evergreen trees that adorn the vicinity of the mansion, and the trim, well-tended grounds that contrast so pleasantly with the wild luxuriance of the surrounding woodlands.

At the neighbouring farm we pick up a track diverging to the left, that leads us over a bridge spanning the lake-like estuary, affording a pretty peep of the mansion upon its bank. Thence our path winds across the breezy slopes of Stackpole Park, until we drop suddenly upon a tiny quay and cluster of cottages, stowed away beside the sea in the oddest corner imaginable, under the sheltering lee of the cliffs. Ensconced in this out-of-the-way nook, we snatch a well-earned *siesta ;* and upon resuming our stroll we follow the coast-line, passing near a cavern that goes by the name of Lort's Cave, and catching a glimpse of the secluded cove of Barrafundle, backed by a stretch of blue sea and the bold crags of Stackpole Head.

Retracing our steps to the farm we pass near a spot where, according to a fading tradition, a certain ghostly party of headless travellers were wont to arrive, about nightfall, in a spectral coach from Tenby ; each pale shade, as 'tis said, bearing his head stowed snugly away under his arm !

Another half-hour sees us into Bosheston, the remotest village of this Ultima Thule. The place has a nautical air all its own ; with a row of trim coastguards' cottages, whose strip of sandy garden ground is embellished with the figure-head of some ' tall Ammiral ' of bygone days. Atop of the hamlet stands the church, a primitive-looking old edifice, with a rude stone cross and broken stoup standing amidst the tombstones. The route is now all plain sailing, for we have merely to ' follow our noses ' along the sandy trackway ; while the salt wind deals us many a lusty buffet as we trudge seawards across the open, shelterless uplands.

Upon reaching the cliff-head, we discover a flight of rough steps, whereof, as the fable goes, no man can tell the number. Descending the winding way we find ourselves, a few minutes later, before St. Govan's Chapel.

This diminutive structure stands in a narrow chine between wild, tumbled crags. It is rudely constructed of weather-stained blocks of limestone, arched over with a primitive kind of vault, and is lighted by two or three narrow windows. A low doorway in the eastern wall gives access to a cell-like recess, just big enough for a man to turn round in. Here, according to a curious old legend, St. Govan sought shelter from his pagan enemies; whereupon the massy rock closed over him and hid him from his pursuers, opening again to release the pious anchorite so soon as the chase was overpassed.

Anent this queer nook, the popular superstition runs that all who can keep to the self-same wish, while they turn around therein, will obtain their desire before the year is out—a belief that, to judge from the well-worn appearance of the rock face, must be widely entertained.

Upon the western gable rises a small bell-cot, long since bereft of its solitary bell. For it happened, 'once upon a time,' that a wicked pirate who chanced to be sailing by became enamoured of its

St Govan's
Chapel

silvery tones, and, landing with his rascally crew, plundered the sanctuary of its treasure. His success, however, was short-lived, for a mighty storm arose and overwhelmed the vessel, so that every soul aboard perished in the raging waves. Meanwhile the bereaved hermit was compensated for his loss with a miraculous stone, which, when struck, gave forth the identical tone of the cherished bell; and credulous folk to this day affirm that the neighbouring rocks ring, upon being struck, with surprising alacrity.

From the chapel we next scramble down to the 'holy well,' a

neglected spot of no interest save such as tradition can lend. Yet in olden times folk were wont to gather here from far and wide, in anticipation of an instant cure for 'those thousand natural shocks that flesh is heir to.'

Quaint legends and superstitions such as these linger, to this day, amongst the older peasantry of this remote portion of South Pembrokeshire. Indeed, the whole locality offers a happy hunting-ground to anyone curious in the matter of old-time folk-lore.

For behold, is not this Gwlâd yr Hûd, the Christian Kymro's Land of Phantasy ; which, long ere the time that history had dawned, was enveloped in Llengêl, the Veil of Mystery ? Each castle-crowned headland of this rock-bound coast, and every grass-grown rath and barrow that furrows the surface of these immemorial hills, has formed the theme of some half-forgotten legend or lingering tradition, long cherished among this imaginative people.

A lonesome, sea-girt land where storms and sea-mists, sweeping from the wide Atlantic, wreath the steadfast hills in unsubstantial vapours, through which each beetling precipice that frowns across the ocean looms like some weird vision of a dream. Amidst such scenes as these, the fantastic creations of the Keltic imagination must readily have found ' a local habitation and a name.'

Well, *revenons à nos moutons,* after this excursion into legend-land. Seated on a mossy stone, we contemplate the age-worn cliffs whose ruddy bastions, carved into a thousand castellated forms, range their impregnable fronts against old Ocean's impetuous artillery. A steady south-westerly breeze sends the green, translucent rollers vollying with thunderous roar against the weed-fringed rocks upon the shore ; while flocks of gulls wheel overhead, drifting on motionless, angular pinions, or sweeping across the breakers with harsh, discordant cries.

We now seek out a view-point for a sketch of the lonely hermitage, a matter of no small difficulty owing to the tumbled nature of the ground ; but eventually we select a sheltered spot where the noontide sun, peering downward from the cloudless vault of heaven, draws out the rich, sweet odours of sea-pink, wild-thyme and gorse.

Mounting again to the brow of the cliffs, we ramble around the lonely coast, which hereabouts is indented with a series of 'crankling nookes' that penetrate, like long fingers, deep into the land.

Here is the wild and perilous abyss yclept the Huntsman's Leap, from the story of some fabulous rider who, putting his horse to full gallop, plunged across the unexpected chasm, only to perish from sheer fright upon regaining his home! The nodding cliffs approach so closely upon either hand, as to have been not inaptly likened to a pair of leviathan vessels locked fast in collision.

A bowshot westward lies Bosheston Meer, a similar cavern sunk fathoms deep in the solid rock. Near it is a funnel-shaped aperture that acts in stormy weather as a blowhole; whence it is said the waves are driven high above the land, plunging back again with a roar that can be heard far inland.

Strange tales were told in bygone times of the freaks of this tempest-torn abyss. George Owen, an Elizabethan chronicler, observes: 'If Sheepe or other like Cattell be grazing neere the Pitt, offtimes they are forcibly and violently Drawne and carryed into the pitt; and if a Cloke, or other garment, bee cast on the grownd neere the Pitt, at certaine seasones, you shall stande afarre off, and see it sodainely snatch'd, drawne and swallowed up into the Pitt, and never seene againe.'

Quitting this wild and fascinating spot, we pass near the grass-grown mounds of a prehistoric camp; and then, striking a little inland, make for a sort of green oasis that marks the 'Sunken Wood.'

A vast, shelving pit, sunk some 50 feet below the level of the ground, and twice as many across, is filled with a grove of vigorous ash-trees. Their dense foliage entirely covers the top of the chasm; where it is cut off, smooth as a well-trimmed hedge, by the sea-spray borne upon the gales from the adjacent ocean.

Many conjectures have been formed as to the origin of this re-markable freak of Nature; the most plausible being that, the subsoil having been excavated by the waves through some subterranean fissure, the ground has fallen in from above and formed this cavity.

We now hark back to the cliffs once more, and coast around the broad inlet of Bullslaughter Bay, whose rocky walls are pierced with many a dark, weed-fringed cavern where

' Old Triton blows his wreathèd horn.'

Pacing the springy turf of the open down, we feast our eyes upon the sparkling waters of the Channel, whose sunlit waves roll in upon the rocky headlands, 'where the broad ocean leans against the land.' The flat, featureless character of the landward view enhances by contrast the attractions of the iron-bound coast ; upon whose wild, fantastic crags and beetling precipices, the traveller gazes in undivided admiration.

Anon we diverge seawards again, and, traversing the grassy mounds of a prehistoric camp, we look down into the depths of a profound abyss known as the Cauldron. The weather-stained precipices of this magnificent chasm rise sheer from the ocean, inaccessible save to the gulls and cormorants that haunt their rocky ledges. Huge archways and vaulted passages, yawning in the limestone rock, afford glimpses of the foam-flecked waves beleaguering, in unceasing onslaught, these sea-girt bulwarks of the steadfast land.

Onward we plod, until erelong the incessant clang and clamour of the myriad sea-fowl that, time out of mind, have made their home amidst these wild and inaccessible sea-cliffs, tell of our approach to the far-famed Stack Rocks.

Standing upon a rocky vantage-point, we have the two lofty, isolated rocks, or 'stacks,' full in view ; rising from the surging ocean that rolls in foaming eddies around their feet. Countless sea-birds wheel with harsh, discordant cries around their weathered sides ; where every available ledge and cranny of the rocks is peopled with a multitude of feathered bipeds, huddled together close as herrings in a barrel. Here, cheek - by - jowl in sociable good-fellowship, cluster clumsy guillemots (or 'eligugs,' as they call them locally), razorbills, and ridiculous-looking puffins in clerical black and white ; while kittiwakes, sea-pies and dark-green cormorants dart about athwart the waves, or, perched upon some projecting ledge, pursue their morning toilette with the utmost *insouciance.*

The eggs of these birds are of rather peculiar form. Very large at one end and pointed at the other, their sides are curiously flattened ; this nice provision of Nature rendering them less liable to roll off the narrow ledges of the rocks which are their resting-place.

Inexorable time forbids our rambling farther around the trend of the sea-cliffs ; so we reluctantly quit their breezy summits to hie away inland past the lonely chapel of Flimston ; keeping straight ahead through sandy lanes glorified with hedges of golden gorse, and 'the swete bramble floure' of good old Chaucer. Presently we come in sight of the tall steeple of Warren Church on the rise of the hill before us.

A long mile westward from our present road lies Bullibur, where traces of an ancient chapel have been brought to light at a spot to this day known as the 'Church Ways.' Anent the erection of this little edifice, the story runs that, as fast as ever the builders could raise their stones from day to day, the Prince of Darkness came along and demolished their handiwork during the night.

Be that as it may, we now press on to Warren ; whose fine old church has a massive tower and spire, of such lofty height as to form a notable landmark to pilots far away at sea. The tunnel-vaulted nave and porch, with a well-preserved cross in the churchyard, complete the tale of Warren's *notabilia*.

With a final glance around the wide-extended landscape, encircled by a blue stretch of the distant Channel, we shape our course over some rising ground at a place called Cold Comfort—a tantalizing misnomer this torrid afternoon. Our road then winds down the hill to a fresh, clear stream, running through water-meadows where cattle stand knee-deep in the cooling shallows ; and so, crossing Stem Bridge, we enter the confines of the ancient Honour of Pembroke.

Breasting the upward slope, we pass through numerous gates athwart the little-frequented highway, which hereabouts calls for no particular notice, being chiefly remarkable for the amazing and dazzling whiteness of its coating of limestone dust, which, under the glare of the afternoon sun, recalls the parched routes of distant Italy. This brings into play our dark, smoked glasses and the weatherbeaten sketching umbrella, to the huge delectation of the small fry skylarking around the wayside cottage gates.

By-and-by the many-windowed front of Orielton appears amidst the rolling woodlands that cluster around a pretty lakelet lying in the hollow of the vale. There is an old saying that Orielton possesses as many windows as the year has days, and as many doors as days in the month ; but finding the fable tally ill with the apparent size of the

mansion, we propound the conundrum to an old road-mender who explains that a large part of the building was 'throwed down' years ago, when he was 'a bit of a boy.'

At Hundleton two roads diverge near the village green, and, as 'all roads lead to Rome,' either will do for Pembroke ; so we steer as straight a course as we can, the lane winding down beneath overarching trees to a secluded nook where a stream meanders, under deep, ruddy sandstone banks, to lose itself in a salt-water 'pill' that joins the Pennar River.

Traversing the long, tedious street of Monkton, our lengthening shadows point the way as we push on once more into Pembroke town ; conjuring up, after the long day's tramp, rare visions of the good cheer awaiting us at the modest quarters where we come to anchor for the night.

AT RHOSCROWTHER

CHAPTER V.

TO ANGLE, RHOSCROWTHER, AND THE CASTLE MARTIN COUNTRY.

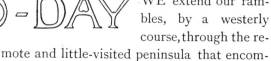 WE extend our rambles, by a westerly course, through the remote and little-visited peninsula that encompasses the 'lardg and spatious Harborough' of Milford Haven, upon its southern flank.

There is an Eastern saying that 'men grow blind in gazing at the sun, and never see the beauty of the stars.' Throughout the locality in question we shall not be dazzled by grand or striking scenery; yet we may happen unawares upon many a nook of pleasant verdure amidst its rolling sandstone hills; and quiet corners, full of an indescribable charm, in the world-forgetting villages (undiscovered by the guide-books) that nestle in its remote, sequestered vales.

Getting away 'bright and early' from Pembroke streets, while the smoke of newly-kindled fires still hangs softly around the old house-tops of the town, the keen, crisp air of the half-awakened day sends us spinning along at a pace that makes short work of the tedious highway.

At a bend of the road we digress into a hollow seductive lane that meanders, in nonchalant fashion, around the head of a tidal inlet; thence our by-way beguiles us, by moss-grown stepping-stones, across a tinkling rill that wantons in rippling eddies amidst big red sandstone boulders, where ivy and hartstongue fern have made their home. Onwards we pursue this secluded lane, under the cool shade of an overhanging coppice; here the deep, ruddy soil is shot with purple hues, from the blue sky mirrored in each shallow puddle left by last night's rain.

In every shadowy nook wreaths of fairy gossamer glisten, like frosted silver, amidst the emerald green of the hedgerow. The merry pipe of linnet and piefinch sounds cheerily forth as we pass along; while that quaint little fellow, the nuthatch, utters his unmistakeable note (resembling the ring of skates on the ice), as he flits from tree to tree. Working his way head-downwards, in his own peculiar fashion, he searches trunk and branches for his favourite fare; striking with his long, sturdy beak, and steadying himself by the purchase of his outspread tail.

Now and again we catch a glimpse of a smart goldfinch, and presently discover his pretty nest, with eggs lying warm and cosy; while sober little wrens flit briskly in and out under the bushes. Even the nightingale, though a *rara avis* in these parts, has, this phenomenal season, been heard in the woods near Cresselly. The following tradition explains how these little songsters came to shun the county of Pembroke. It appears that St. David, 'being seriously occupied in the night tyme in his diverse orizons, was soe troubled with the swete tuninges of the Nightingall as that he praied unto th' Almightie that, from that tyme forward, there might never a Nightingall sing within his Dioces; and this was the cause of confininge of the bird out of this countrey. Thus much,' remarks the chronicler, 'to recreat the reader's spirettes.'

Presently as we rise the hill a broad, land-locked bay opens out to the briny Haven at Pennar Mouth. In the words of that quaint chronicler, George Owen: 'This is the creke that cometh upp to Pembroke towne. It is the largest and greatest creke of al Milforde, and passeth upp into the land a three Myle and more; and at the upper End it parteth itself in two Branches, and compasseth about the Towne and castle of Pembroke; serving the said Towne for a moate, or strong Ditch, on every side thereof. A Bark of 40 or 50 Tonnes may enter this Creke att low water, and ride at Ankher att Crowpoole, but noe further without helpe of ye Tyde. The Crow is a shallow, or shelf, a pretty way within the entrance of Pennar; on itt groweth the best Oysters of Milforde. It is a big and sweete Oyster,' saith he, 'and poore folk gather them without dredging.'

Far away upon the glassy waters of the Haven, a handful of vessels lie at anchor off Hobb's Point, where the old coach-road runs down to the ferry. All this is soon lost to view as we descend to a tree-shaded dingle, aglow with foxgloves, campion and yellow *fleur-de-lys*. Anon our path winds upwards across an open hillside, amidst acres of glowing gorse; passing a few lonely thatched cottages, with donkeys browsing leisurely about their open doors.

At a place called Wallaston Cross five lanes converge, necessitating a consultation with the trusty Ordnance map. The choice falls upon an upland road, running along the brow of a hill, that raises us just high enough to peep across the Haven to Milford town, and the towers of distant Pembroke; over which we catch a glimpse of the Precelly hills, lying far away upon the northern horizon.

Down in a sequestered dell, overlooking the estuary, nestles the little church of Pwllcroghan; its low tower and dumpy spire scarce out-topping a grove of tempest-torn trees.

Long ago this lowly edifice was restored by Ralph de Beneger, a former Rector, whose counterfeit presentment reposes in his church beneath a canopy bearing the inscription: 'Hic jacet Radulphus Beneger, hujus ecclesiæ Rector.' In 1648 a skirmish took place in Pwllcroghan churchyard, between the Royalist and Parliamentary troops; when it is recorded that 'the malignants, as was their custom, displayed on their hats the legend, " We long to see our King." '

Trudging steadily onwards, we pass near Hênllan House, formerly a possession of the Whites of Tenby; a place which still keeps its old Welsh name amidst all its Saxon neighbours. That rascally vagrant the cuckoo now pipes up from a neighbouring coppice, and 'tells his name to all the hills' in monotonous iteration; while lovely Silverwashed Fritillaries and sky-blue butterflies flit to and fro beside the hedgerow.

At a crook of the lane we turn through a gate, and follow the ' foredraught' down to Eastington farmhouse, where the good-natured farmer and his better-half provide bed and board for the coming night; a vast convenience in this unfrequented district, which offers no accommodation of a higher type than the ordinary hedge alehouse.

After despatching a modest repast, in which the staff of life forms the backbone of our fare, we resume our devious ramble. An unmistakeable footpath leads past the ruins of a deserted water-mill to the shore of Angle Bay, whose calm blue waters, spreading broadly into the land, mirror a cloudless sky of unrivalled purity. Skirting an ancient moss-grown wall which, for some inscrutable reason, encloses a tract of apparently valueless marshland, we roam across the shingly beach towards a group of isolated buildings. Pale yellow sea-poppies, taking heart of grace to brave the lusty breezes, beautify the waste places with their delicate flowers; and groups of cattle, standing knee-deep in the shallows, add a touch of life to the pleasant, tranquil scene.

Our route now lies around the rocky shore, an opportune fieldpath skirting the low cliffs, and affording lovely ever-changing views over the sunny landscape and the land-locked Haven. The warm south wind, sweet from clover fields, is fraught with the roar of the ocean, driving full into Freshwater Bay a mile away beyond the sandy burrows; but here under the lee of the hill, scarce a breath of air stirs the ripening barley. Suddenly a brace of partridges blusters away from the sun-baked ploughfield, where the ruddy eye of the 'pimpernel' peeps from every furrow.

Ensconced beneath a gnarled old hawthorn hedge wreathed in fragrant woodbine, we indulge in a quiet pipe; watching the rabbits as they scuttle to and fro under the sandy bank, and the dainty blue dragonflies hovering over the meadowsweet and ragged Robin, that deck the oozy course of the streamlet at our feet. The deep tones of a steamer's syren float across the water, followed by the report of a heavy gun from a fortress guarding the Haven; for the summer manœuvres are now in full swing, and we can see the white-peaked tents of the Connaught Rangers behind Angle Point.

The gracefully curving shore is fringed with a broad stretch of seaweed, of every hue from golden brown to bottle green, whence the pungent odour of ozone is borne upon the sun-warmed air.

Glancing back across the bay, we catch a glimpse of the old farm-house that is to be our local habitation for to-night; near which the tower of Rhôscrowther Church rises amidst its solitary grove of trees.

A long mile further we enter the village of Angle (or Nangle, as it is sometimes called), a place that in ancient deeds is styled 'in Angulo,' doubtless from its situation in a *corner* of the land.

The long village street with its one-storied cottages, many of them coloured yellow, pink or blue, and all embowered in luxuriant climbing plants, has a pleasant, cheery look; and as we advance a ruined tower comes into view, rising above some marshy meadows beside the stream. This is all that remains of the castle of Angle, once the abode of the Sherbornes, an ancient family in the land, who were formerly lords of Angle. At no great distance from the church are some remains of a handsome structure of uncertain antiquity. Nothing is known about the history of these ruins; but they have supplied a peg whereon to hang a local legend, somewhat to the following effect: 'Once upon a time,' three sisters and co-heiresses, finding they could not pull together under the same roof, agreed to build each of them a dwelling for herself. The first is said to have erected the castle; the second, the curious old house above mentioned; and the third, a mansion just without the village, where a house named Hall now stands.

Turning through a wicket-gate, we pass by an old stone cross and enter the church, over which, alas! has swept the moloch of modern restoration, obliterating much of its original character. In one corner, however, we espy a queer little organ of primitive type, with unenclosed pipes and keyboard, not unlike the spinet of earlier days. This has been recently evicted in favour of a brand-new instrument designed by the present vicar, who is skilled in the art and mystery of organ-building.

Angle Church was one of the numerous benefices held by that famous Welsh chronicler, Giraldus Cambrensis.

In a corner of the churchyard, overlooking the tidal inlet, rises a picturesque little chapel frequented in olden times by the seafaring folk, when embarking upon or returning from their ventures on the vasty deep. Externally all is obscured beneath a mantle of glossy green ivy, save where a traceried window or low-arched doorway peeps from under the shadowy foliage. Ascending a few steps to the interior, we find ourselves in a small, oblong chamber covered with a pointed stone vault; at the east end stands a plain, stone altar, surmounted by an elegant little traceried window, whose modern painted glass portrays Scriptural scenes appropriate to the purpose of the chapel.

SEAMENS CHAPEL
AT ANGLE.

A small piscina, and the recumbent figure of some unknown ecclesiastic under an arched recess, adorn this nutshell of a church. Beneath it is a crypt of similar dimensions, entered through a doorway at the eastern end, and lighted by small quatrefoil openings pierced through the thickness of the walls.

We now turn our attention to the castle ruins, which are reached by passing the school-house and crossing a small grass-plot, adorned with a simple monument to some local benefactor.   Little else remains besides a tall, ivy-clad peel-tower, whose massive limestone walls abut upon the shallow stream that meanders to the bay.   These solid walls are honeycombed with archways and passages ; while a good, stone-newel stairway corkscrews up to the outermost battlements, above

Ruined Castle at Angle

which rises a circular chimney-shaft.   Each of the four stories had its own fireplace, window recesses and other conveniences ; and the lower chamber is stoutly vaulted with stone.   Altogether, the place appears to have been built in such a self-contained fashion as to be capable of resisting attack, or even sustaining a siege.

Close at hand stands a low, rambling, yellow-washed house, having every sign of age about it. Many years ago this was the Castle Inn. The interior shows dark, open-raftered ceilings, where mighty hams and flitches of bacon ripen the year round; broad-beamed oaken chairs flank a solid table standing upon the rough, flagged floor; while dogs, cats, hens and chickens roam sociably everywhere. A carved stone head, peeping out from amidst the honeysuckle that clambers over the porch, is *said* to represent Giraldus Cambrensis himself, a statement that must be accepted with the proverbial 'grain of salt.'

The rough outbuildings at the rear also bear traces of antiquity; and in an adjacent meadow stands one of those curious old pigeon-houses, which formed a customary adjunct to the mediæval castle or manor-house. The thick stone walls of this pigeon-house are built in a circular form, surmounted by a high conical roof much the worse (except from a picturesque point of view) for several centuries of neglect and hard weather; the interior is pierced with many tiers of pigeon-holes, each with a ledge for the bird to rest upon, while an 'eye' in the crown of the roof served its feathered inmates as a doorway. The original arched entrance has been broken away to form a larger opening, and the whole structure appears to be coëval with the neighbouring castle. This pigeon-house appears in our sketch of Angle Castle.

Invigorated by a crisp sea-breeze that drives the fleecy clouds before it, we put our best foot foremost, and stretch away along a rough cart-lane between banks of prickly furze and stunted hawthorn hedges. These give place, after passing a solitary farmstead, to the open, wind-swept down, aglow with amber-tinted gorse, and carpeted with dry, crisp turf and tussocks of flowering thrift.

Half a mile across this bracing moorland lands us at the old ruined Blockhouse, built, as George Owen informs us, in the days of Henry VIII. 'for to ympeach the entrance into the Haven.' Hence we look out across the open seaway, that forms a worthy approach to the noble estuary of Milford Haven.

From this sea-girt eyrie we command a spacious outlook over land and sea. Standing beside the gray, lichen-clad ruins of the old watch-tower, our gaze wanders across a sparkling expanse of open sea that rolls, in waves of clearest aquamarine and sapphire blue, towards the land-locked shelter of the Haven; and breaks into crests of snowy foam where St. Anne's Head stands out and takes the brunt of old Ocean's fury. The ruddy, sandstone rocks rise in picturesque confusion from the surging breakers, which eddy around a tiny islet accessible only at low tide; whose forefront, planted in the ocean, is barbed with a grim array of jagged ledges and pierced with dark, yawning crevices.

Beyond West Angle Bay the mainland rounds away eastwards, with a fort-crowned islet protecting the inner reaches of the famous estuary.

It is to be hoped that the unrivalled advantages of Milford Haven will ere long be turned to better account. With its noble fairway, un-trammelled by shoal or bar, and deep, land-locked reaches where the whole British Navy might safely ride at anchor, Milford Haven has no compeer along our western seaboard. Given a better system of railway communication, and proper facilities in the way of docks and wharves, Milford should, in days to come, stand *facile princeps* as a seaport for the magnificent vessels engaged in the great and ever-increasing traffic of the Atlantic ' ferry.'

But, meanwhile, time is stealing a march upon us, and the lengthen-ing shadows warn us to depart; so, casting a last glance across the sunlit sea, flecked with white 'mares'-tails' and dotted with brown-sailed trawlers, we retrace our track over the breezy headland. At every step we inhale the healthful smell of wave-washed seaweed, and tread underfoot the flowers that gem the rough, uneven ground—thrift, trefoil, blue sheep's bit and a minute, starlike flower whose name we do not know.

Pushing on through the quiet street of Angle, we diverge up a steep, shady lane in search of Bangeston House; which proves to be nothing more than the gaunt, dismantled walls of a vast group of buildings, apparently of early eighteenth-century date, mantled in ivy and over-shadowed by sombre trees. The ruins cover a large extent of ground, and appear to have been regarded by the neighbours as a convenient quarry for building materials. Bangeston was, as its name implies, the ancestral home of the Benegers, a family of much consequence in olden times who possessed broad acres hereabouts, but whose very name has long since become extinct.

Curious tales of the former occupants of Bangeston still linger amongst the cottagers. A certain Lord Lyon, the Garter King-at-Arms of his time, is said to have dwelt here many years ago; and an ancient graybeard whom we meet volunteers the information that, 'It was a gret plaäce in they times, and I've a-heared tell as there was quare doings when Lord Lyon lived in th' ould marnsion. It was him as drove with a coach and horses, one dirty night, and went right over the clift (they do say), down by Freshwater way, and was never seed again.'

JESTYNTON.

Much edified by the yarns of Old Mortality, we now retrace our steps to Eastington Farm; musing meanwhile over these fast-fading fables, and meeting a few belated peasant-folk trudging home through the gray of the gloaming.

Eastington, or more properly Jestynton, is traditionally reputed to have been, in days long before the Conquest, the abode of Jestyn, grandson of Howel Ddâ, Prince of South Wales. A descendant of his, whose unpronounceable name we refrain from recording, was married to Sir Stephen Perrot, the first Norman of that name to settle in this

13

county; who by this alliance acquired vast possessions and influence throughout all the countryside.

This quaint old homestead of Eastington, under whose hospitable roof we spend the night, is honeycombed with curious nooks and corners, that lure us on to endless scrambles amidst dark, crooked passages, and crumbling stairways. The long south front, with its homely porch and small-paned windows, is flanked at its western end by a massive mediæval structure whose rough, lichen-clad walls are pierced with narrow, deep-set windows, and topped by ruinous battlements; all looking so hoary and ancient, one is disposed to fancy this may be a remnant of the royal residence of that old Welsh Prince whose name it bears.

By a rude, steep flight of grass-grown steps we mount to a clumsy door, that swings noisily on its crazy hinges as we push our way into the interior. We now find ourselves in a large and lofty chamber, whose solid, concrete floor is prettily marked out with lines traced in simple geometrical patterns. Rudely-arched windows admit light at either end, one of them having cusped openings; while a ruined fire-place yawns in the centre of the opposite wall.

A small vaulted cell opens from one end of this room; and a narrow stair, winding through the thickness of the wall, ascends to the battlemented roof, which has a gangway all around and is pierced with loopholes for defence. The dark, vaulted basement of this ancient fabric forms a capital cool dairy, where mine hostess shows us with pardonable pride her clean, earthenware pans brimful of the freshest of fresh milk and cream.

Anon ensues a quiet chat over the evening pipe; the mellowing flitches forming a canopy overhead as we lounge in the cavernous chimney-corner. At last we retire to our lowly chamber, to be serenaded far into the night by the boom of heavy guns, waging mimic warfare by land and sea; while the glare of electric search-lights turns night into noontide, in a highly distracting fashion.

Next morning the heavens are already as brass above our heads when, turning our backs on Jestynton, we strike into the meadow-path that leads down to Rhôscrowther village. Ensconced in a secluded dell remote from the busy haunts of men, this quiet hamlet has a look of rest and fair contentment; yet the place must have been of no little importance in bygone times, for there is reason to believe that the Bishop of St. Davids had one of his seven palaces in this parish.

Down in a hollow beside the stream stands the ancient parish church, dedicated to St. Decumanus, patron of springs and wells, who in olden times was held in high esteem for the cures effected at the bubbling rill hard by.

This venerable church remains pretty much in its original condition, and presents a picturesque array of roofs and gables, clustering beneath its tall gray tower. The gable of the nave is crowned by a pretty bell-cot, which probably did duty prior to the erection of the tower. The latter is a stout old structure with 'battered' or sloping walls, having both an inner and an outer roof of stone, and looking as though built with a view to defence.

The north porch is unusually spacious. Its broad gable end is adorned with the arms of the Daws of Bangeston, and the badge of the Whites of Hentland, a notable family in bygone days, whose chapel is in the north transept. Alongside the arched doorway of the porch is a square-headed opening, supposed to have been used as an alms window, through which, in those easy-going times, the priest handed out the dole of bread, money or what not to his *protégés.*

Our attention is next attracted by a diminutive figure surmounting the arch of the inner entrance. Upon closer inspection this archaic image appears to be seated, with the right hand raised in the attitude of benediction. It was rescued, we understand, many years ago from the iconoclastic restorers who were then working their will on Angle Church; and was placed in its present position by the Rector of this parish.

Upon entering into the sacred edifice, its picturesque proportions excite our admiration. Notwithstanding its modest dimensions the short transepts, curious angle passages and chancel with its pretty aisle, give a quaint, varied look to the low interior.

The north wall of the chancel is adorned with a handsome,

crocketed canopy, which terminates in a triplet of queer, sculptured faces symbolical of the Holy Trinity. This monument partly hides an ancient niche or aumbry, where the wafer was probably kept in pre-Reformation times. The adjacent south aisle has two canopied recesses ; under one of which reposes the handsome, though somewhat damaged, effigy of a lady, with a wimple over her chin such as is worn to this day in the northern part of the county. The wall above is pierced

AC RHÔSCROWTHER

with a small piscina arch ; and the chamber is lighted by windows of very good Pembrokeshire type.

This aisle is known as the Jestyn-ton Chapel, from the mansion of that ilk to which it still appertains ; and there is a tradition that Jestyn, Prince of South Wales, built the church ; placing it conveniently near to his own residence, though remote from the rest of the parish.

Many other interesting features will reward a diligent search ; and the visitor who is curious in such matters will notice that the chancel arch has evidently been cut through from the earlier nave. The south doorway, abandoned in favour of the more sheltered north porch, affords a con-

venient niche for the font ; while odd corners here and there conceal old tombstones, inscribed with quaint epitaphs or half-obliterated armorial scutcheons.

In passing through the churchyard, we examine a dilapidated cross, remarkable for a circular hole in the base supposed to have been used as a receptacle for contributions to the priest from his flock. Near the adjacent stile stands an ancient, upright stone inscribed with curious, illegible characters.

At the little foot-bridge spanning the stream, we halt to enjoy a pleasant retrospect of the time-honoured church, set amidst embowering trees, with a handful of lowly cottages scattered prettily around.

Thence we push on by a footpath across the upland meadows; climbing stone stiles, set in the turfy walls which do duty here as hedgerows. Gradually we ascend to the wind-swept plateau at Newton; and if the ascent is easily won, it is none the less worth winning; for it affords an ample outlook over land and sea, with the village of Castle Martin upon the rise of the opposite hill.

Our track now becomes somewhat obscure, so we call in to inquire the way at the neighbouring blacksmith's shop; when a soot-begrimed son of Vulcan, casting aside his hammer, good-naturedly pioneers us along an intricate by-way, and points out the bearings for crossing the marshy valley. A wild enough place is this in winter-time, as our guide can testify; where the very hayricks have to be lashed secure to weather the fierce sou'-westers, which, under their steady impact, bend the trees into strange, distorted forms.

Descending the rough braeside, we now make for a conspicuous old ash-tree, and thenceforward thread our way amidst the dykes and marshy levels of Castle Martin Corse.

The tall steeple of Warren church, showing clear against the sky ahead, makes a serviceable landmark, until we strike the grassy track that leads across the marsh. Arrayed in sombre hues of russet red, rich browns and olive greens, the level strath is dotted with groups of horses and the black cattle for which the locality is famed, grazing knee-deep amidst waving sedges and lush green water-plants.

As we advance, the lapwings (those lovers of lonely, unfrequented places), wheel and circle overhead, uttering their peculiarly plaintive pipe as they scan the unwelcome intruders. And now a hollow lane receives us, and keeps us company until, after passing a two-three humble tenements, we turn aside into the well-tended graveyard; and so to the parish church of St. Michael, which stands in a little elbow of the hill overlooking the scattered dwellings of the hamlet.

Castle Martin church has made so doughty a stand against the

ravages of time that now, in its green old age, it presents an extremely
picturesque appearance as we approach its weather-beaten portal.
Before passing within, let us pause awhile to scan the features of this
characteristic old Pembrokeshire church.

Prominent in our view rises the gray limestone tower, whose

CASTLE MARTIN
CHURCH

rugged, time-worn walls rise solidly to the corbelled battlements.
These have louvred windows to the bell-chamber, and a quaint metal
weather-vane atop; to right and left range the lichen-clad roofs and
walls of the main structure; while a lofty and massive porch stands
boldly out, enclosing a rambling stairway that leads to the tower.   The

foreground is occupied by crumbling headstones, wreathed in ivy and decked with flowering creepers ; and a shapely churchyard cross rises beside our pathway.

Nor does the interior of the church prove a whit less interesting. Here a group of graceful arches, with attached limestone shafts, gives access from the nave to the north aisle; whence a skew arch, having detached pillars with capitals, opens into the chancel. The latter is flanked by similar arches enclosing pretty, traceried windows.

The great south porch has a narrow doorway at some height in the side wall, giving access to a much-worn, straggling flight of steps. Scrambling up these we find ourselves in the tower, which, after the manner of the country, is massively constructed ; having grim vaulted chambers with many openings, like pigeon-holes, pierced in the solid walls. Here are also the bells, erected by John Rudhale, A.D. 1809. The font, though plain, is well proportioned and of early date.

This curious old church is the head of the important parish and hundred of Castle Martin. The district is noted for its breed of black, long-horned cattle ; and in bygone days could boast its own troop of gallant yeomanry, who shared with the Fishguard Fencibles the distinction of repelling the notorious French 'invasion' of Pembrokeshire, a century ago.

Leaving the quiet village to the care of an aged crone and a group of children playing with a lame magpie, we get under way again, and make for the crossways on the ridge. At this point the Ordnance map raises expectations of something of a 'castle,' which proves, however, to be nothing more than a prehistoric earthwork with mounds of circular form. Then onward again, passing Moor Farm, where once stood a goodly mansion, of which scarce a stone has been spared. Now we keep a straight course towards Warren, with the skylarks making music overhead; while the voice of that 'interesting scamp,' the cuckoo, echoes from the woods down Brownslade way.

Shortly before reaching Warren village the country lane widens out, with a corner of sedgy greensward under the hedgerow. Here stands a curious old wayside well, domed over with a sort of rude canopy, whose mossy stones, fringed with hartstongue fern, are reflected in the clear water ; indeed, from the frequent recurrence of

springs and draw-wells, it would seem that St. Decumanus, their patron, was held in high esteem in these parts.

At Warren we call a halt to refresh the 'inner man ;' then lounge awhile in a shady nook, for a chat and a quiet pipe. Towards the cool of evening we bear away for distant Pembroke, by the road that leads past Orielton, where we are on familiar ground which has been touched upon in describing a previous route.

A WAYSIDE WELL.

CASTLE MARTIN

CHAPTER VI.

CAREW, WITH ITS CROSS, CASTLE AND CHURCH. UPTON CASTLE AND
CHAPEL. PEMBROKE DOCK AND HAVERFORDWEST.

SETTING FORTH by the morning train, we alight at Lamphey Station; whence we make our way to the grand old ruins of Carew Castle, as our *pièce de résistance* for to-day. Once free of Lamphey village, we soon find ourselves striding across the Ridgeway by Lamphey Park; whence we get a pretty retrospect, under some weatherbeaten trees, of the pleasant vale we have quitted, with a more distant peep of the towers of Pembroke Castle. Here, too, we find a few traces of olden times in a group of gray, weather-stained farm-buildings; remnants, maybe, of Bishop Vaughan's famous grange.

At Rambler's Folly, on the crest of the ridge, we get the first glimpse of our destination, down in the valley below; with a background of open country rolling upward to the distant hills; while, by taking the trouble to cross over the road, we command the broad plain of the sea.

A shepherd with collie-dog at heel, driving his flock to pasture, now puts us in the way of a short-cut across the meadows. This woodland path is enlivened by a bevy of butterflies that, like ourselves, are taking the morning air. Here floats a stately 'peacock,' while yonder sprightly Atalanta, perched upon a spray of woodbine, displays her becoming *toilette* of scarlet and glossy black, edged with daintiest lace.

Approaching our destination, we skirt around a marshy watercourse

14

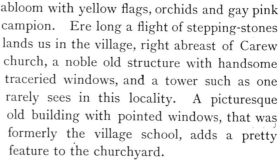

abloom with yellow flags, orchids and gay pink campion. Ere long a flight of stepping-stones lands us in the village, right abreast of Carew church, a noble old structure with handsome traceried windows, and a tower such as one rarely sees in this locality. A picturesque old building with pointed windows, that was formerly the village school, adds a pretty feature to the churchyard.

But we must push on to the castle, reserving these minor matters for future investigation. Half a mile of hard highroad ensues, when, just before the castle gate is reached, our attention is absorbed by an object standing upon the steep bank, hard by the road.

This is Carew Cross, a hoary monument before whose patriarchal antiquity the ruined castle is little better than a mere *parvenu.* The huge monolith of lichen-clad stone terminates in a circular head enclosing a Celtic cross ; while each of the four sides is richly overlaid with deeply-incised patterns, carved in that curious, interlacing fashion peculiar to these early monuments. The date of its erection is placed as far back as the ninth century : upon its eastern face is seen a rudely-fashioned cross, each limb of which is formed by three deeply-cut lines ; while the reverse side is inscribed with certain archaic characters, which some ingenious antiquary has interpreted thus :

THE CROSS OF THE SON OF ILTEUT THE SON OF ECETT.

Having completed the sketch of Carew Cross, which figures on the opposite page, we now pass on to view the wonders of the castle.

Carew Castle is located in a district which from very early times formed a royal appanage of the princes of South Wales. It was presented as a marriage dower with the fair Nesta, daughter of Rhys ap Tydwr, to Gerald de Windsor, the King's castellan, in the reign of Henry I. This great demesne was subsequently mortgaged by Sir Edward de Carew to the gallant Sir Rhys ap Thomas, by whom the castle appears to have been largely remodelled. Here it was that this doughty Welshman entertained his liege the Earl of Richmond, on his way from Milford to victorious Bosworth field; placing the royal arms, in memory of the event, upon a chimney-piece in the chamber where 'the hope of England' slept.

In olden times Carew Castle was surrounded by an extensive chase, or deer park. Here in 1507 Sir Rhys ap Thomas held 'a solemn just and turnament for the honour of St. George, patrone of that noble Order of the Garter,' when Henry VII. honoured the revels with his presence. A full account of this 'princelie fête' has been preserved, setting forth how 'manie valerouse gentlemen' then made trial of their abilities ' in feates of armes, the men of prime Ranke being lodged within the Castle, others of good Qualitie in tents and Pavilions, pitched in the Parke.'

This 'Festivall and time of jollytie' commenced on the day dedicated to 'the trustie Patrone and protector of Marshalistes,' and continued for five whole days; the tournament taking place on the fourth day, when Sir William Herbert was the challenger, the lord of Carew playing the judge's part.

To the credit of all concerned it is recorded that, throughout all these 'justes and turnaments, seasoned with a diversitie of musicke for the honoure of Ladyes,' in spite of ' knockes valerouslie received and manfullie bestowed, among a thousand people there was not one Quarrell, crosse worde or unkinde Looke, that happened betweene them.'

Wonderful stories were told of the feats of arms performed by the doughty Sir Rhys ap Thomas; insomuch that for years after his day

the name of Sir Rhys ap Thomas was 'used about Terwin as a bugg-
beare or fire Abbaas, such as Talbott's was in Henrie the Sixt's time,
to affright the children from doing shrewd Trickes.'   It is related how
Sir Rhys, mounted on his veteran charger Grey Fetlocks, contrived
to run the impostor Perkin Warbeck to earth at the monastery of
Beaulieu, in Hampshire; and was rewarded for this gallant service by
receiving the Order of the Garter from his sovereign.   At the Battle
of the Spurs this stout-hearted warrior led the light horse and archers
against the enemy, and took the Duke of Longueville prisoner with his
own hands.

Shortly after this event, having attained the age of threescore
years, this brave old knight at last hung up his well-worn weapons in
his Castle of Carew.   Sir Rhys spent his declining days in extending
and beautifying the stately fabric ; calling in to his aid, we may be sure,
the advice of his friend and neighbour the talented Bishop Vaughan,
then dwelling at Lamphey Palace.   Finally, after considerably over-
passing the allotted span, Sir Rhys ap Thomas was gathered to his
fathers in the year of grace 1527.

Meanwhile, traversing a broad green meadow, we approach the
ivy-wreathed walls and turrets of the castle.   This magnificent edifice
is built around a large central courtyard.   It has a huge bastion at
each corner and displays, even in its dismantled condition, a most
interesting combination of military and domestic architecture.

Before us rises the gate-house, probably the oldest portion of the
present building.   An adjacent tower contains the chapel, dating from
Edwardian times and retaining its groined ceiling ; and in one of the
upper chambers we notice a fireplace bearing what appear to be the
arms of Spain.   The fragment of a graceful oriel is seen high aloft in
the wall as we pass under the barbican tower, a massive structure
with vaulted archways, portcullis and machicolated battlements.

We now emerge upon the inner courtyard of the castle, whose
broad expanse of velvety turf is overshadowed on every side by gray
old limestone walls, pierced with pointed doorways and many-mullioned
windows.

The most prominent feature here is the ivy-clad portal of the banqueting-hall. This picturesque structure rises through two stories, and is adorned with some crumbling scutcheons, charged with the insignia of Henry of Richmond and of Sir Rhys ap Thomas; combined with the hoary, time-worn architecture of the banqueting-hall, the whole forms a charming subject for the artist's pencil.

A CORNER OF CAREW CASTLE

The banqueting-hall itself must have been a magnificent apartment. It still shows traces of rich Gothic ornamentation in the deep recesses of its arched windows, doorways and huge fireplaces; while the springing of the open-timbered roof can be readily discerned. In another direction is seen the incomparable range of lofty, mullioned windows of the broad north front. This grandiose *façade* was begun, but never completed, by Sir John Perrot : it contains a sumptuous state-room, over 100 feet in length, and numerous smaller apartments.

An hour vanishes in next to no time as we ramble amidst these echoing chambers, and clamber up and down the broken stairways. Here we pry into some deep, dark dungeon ; yonder, peer through a narrow lancet ; and anon mount to the crumbling battlements, to the no small dismay of a host of jackdaws that haunt these ruined walls. Meanwhile imagination re-peoples these deserted halls and desolate

CAREW CASTLE

chambers with those throngs of faire ladyes, and gallant knights and squires, those troops of servitors and men-at-arms, and all the countless on-hangers that went to swell the princely *ménage* of its mediæval masters.

Presently we pass out again, to wander around the brave old fortress and mark the gaping breaches wrought by Cromwell's cannon, what time the beleaguered garrison fought for King Charles I., holding out long and valiantly until, Tenby having succumbed, Carew at length fell a prize to the Parliamentary arms. The accompanying sketch shows that most of the south front has been demolished, thus giving us a glimpse of the internal courtyard and a portion of the lofty northern *façade*.

Upon quitting the castle we stroll across the neighbouring bridge, whence we obtain a noble view of the great north front with its lofty oriels and vast, mullioned windows reflected in the shallow waters of the tideway. Our appearance upon the scene disturbs a meditative heron, who, pulling himself together, spreads his broad wings and stretches away in leisurely flight to more secluded quarters.

Pausing as we pass for another glance at the ancient Cross, we now retrace our steps to the village to complete our investigations there.

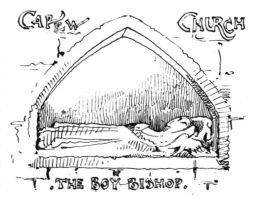

Arrived at the church, we prowl around that sacred edifice ; noting its lofty Perpendicular tower, fine traceried windows and stair-turret surmounted by a low spirelet; then we pass within, and proceed to look about us.

The interior of Carew Church is unusually lofty and spacious, comprising nave with aisles, chancel and transepts. Lofty, well-proportioned limestone arches open into the latter, their piers embellished with the four-leaved flower that marks the artistic influence of Bishop Gower.

The chancel contains a pretty sedilia and piscina, arched in the wall; while an adjacent niche is tenanted by a curious little figure carved in stone, and supposed to commemorate a certain boy-bishop, elected, according to a quaint old custom, from amongst his fellow-choristers.

Be that as it may, we now turn to the opposite wall where, beneath plain, pointed recesses repose the figures of an ecclesiastic habited as a monk, and a knight in armour, sword in hand and shield upon arm, legs crossed at the knees, and head and·feet supported by carven animals.   The latter is a finely-executed piece of sculpture, and withal remarkable from the disproportionate size of the head, which is twisted

Old Rectory House at Carew

in a strange man- ner over the right shoulder—perhaps a personal trait com- mitted to marble.

Whom these figures represent is not precisely known, but we may reason- ably hazard the con- jecture that this mail-clad effigy re- presents some for- gotten scion of the noble family of Carew, erstwhile lords of this place.

The ancient tiles upon the chancel floor are also worthy of notice, displaying the emblems of the bishopric with the arms of Sir Rhys ap Thomas, the Tudor rose, and various other devices.

Having completed our survey of this interesting church, we next make our way to a curious-looking structure known as the Old Rectory. Though now a mere farm-house the place bears traces of considerable antiquity, and appears, like many of the older dwellings in this locality, to have been built with an eye to defence. The massive walls are corbelled out beneath the eaves of the roof, which is pitched at a steep angle, giving the old structure a picturesque appearance. The house has apparently been formerly enclosed within a walled precinct ; and a fast-fading tradition tells vaguely of 'the soldiers' having been quartered here in the turbulent days of old.

But it is high time to be up and away, so pulling ourselves together we face the slanting sunlight, and put the best foot foremost *en route* for Upton Castle.

After passing the grounds of Milton House, we follow the Pem-

UPTON CASTLE.

broke road for about a mile and a half, until, just short of the finger-post, we strike into a hollow lane that leads direct to Upton. The latter part of the way goes through a shady avenue, affording glimpses of the winding Haven and the broad, gray front of Carew Castle.

Upton Castle is undoubtedly of very ancient origin, but it has been restored and rendered habitable of late years, and is now occupied as a dwelling-house. The original gateway, with its double arch, is flanked by tall round towers pierced with loopholes for archery, and is crowned

15

by corbelled battlements. A small old building beside the neighbouring creek was probably used as a guard-house or watch-tower.

Within the castle grounds stands Upton Chapel, a lowly structure of no architectural pretensions, yet containing several objects well worthy of notice.

Opposite the entrance is the fine mural monument seen on the left of our sketch. The figure beneath the canopy is supposed to represent one of the Malefants, an extinct family that for several centuries made a considerable figure in this and the adjacent counties. The knight is clad in a complete suit of mail, having a chain around the neck, with the hands folded in the attitude of prayer. The upper portion of the monument bears traces of colour and decoration, while the canted ends are adorned with carven figures beneath dainty canopies.

A curious if not unique feature is the candelabrum, in the form of a clenched fist, that projects from the adjacent wall. This singular object is fashioned from a piece of yellow limestone, and is pierced with a hole to contain the candle formerly used at funerals and other ceremonies. It appears probable that the worthy knight whose effigy lies near may have left a small pension for the maintenance of this candelabrum.

The handsome Jacobean pulpit was originally in St. Mary's Church at Haverfordwest, whence it was acquired by purchase during the restoration of that edifice.

Upon passing through the small, plain chancel arch, we espy a huge, dilapidated effigy in a corner by the south wall. Though bereft of half its lower limbs, the figure still measures fully six feet in length. This image is clad in a complete suit of chain-mail, and is considered to be the most ancient of its kind in the county. To its history we have no clue, but tradition avers that this rude specimen of the sculptor's art represents a certain ' tall Ammiral' of bygone times, Lord of Upton Castle, who, returning from distant voyagings, was wrecked and cast lifeless ashore almost within sight of home.

A stone let into the chancel pavement shows the tonsured head of an ecclesiastic, with a floreated cross and damaged inscription. Within the Communion-rails we observe a female figure, draped from head to foot in flowing robes and lying under an ogee canopy. Though devoid of any distinctive badge this figure is well executed, and in a very fair state of preservation.

OLD CHAPEL
AT UPTON
NEAR PEMBROKE

Upon the south side of the chapel, and close to the entrance-door, rises the small stone cross figured at the end of this chapter. It is raised upon a sort of basement constructed of masonry overgrown with vegetation, and is approached by rough stone steps.

We now retrace our steps to the highroad, and at the fingerpost bear to the left. Just beyond the old toll-gate we pass near a house called Holyland, so named from the fact that its stones were drawn from the ruins of an ancient hospital, dedicated to St. Mary Magdalene, which formerly existed at Pembroke.

As we traverse the King's Bridge, at the head of the tidal water, the clamour of the ' many-wintered crows,' winging their homeward flight to a neighbouring spinny, falls pleasantly on our ears. Thus we re-enter the quiet street of Pembroke, while the arrowy swifts, wheeling around St. Mary's timeworn steeple, fill the air with their shrill, piercing cries.

Finally we round off the day's adventures by climbing the castle walls, whence the eye traces all the familiar landmarks standing clear-cut against a glowing sky, with a broad span of the fast-empurpling landscape, locked in a silvery reach of the winding Haven.

    *   *   *   *   *   *

Beside the deep, untroubled waters of Milford Haven, there has grown up within the present century one of the finest and most complete shipbuilding establishments around our coasts. Here were constructed those hearts of oak that bore our flag so bravely in days of yore; and hence are nowadays turned out the leviathan ' battleships ' that will bear the brunt of Britain's future wars upon the vasty deep.

Lord Nelson was, we believe, one of the first to point out the peculiar advantages offered by Milford as a constructing yard for the British navy.

In the first years of the present century, the Government rented an existing yard at Milford for a term of fourteen years; after which, being unable to come to terms with Lady Mansfield's representatives, the authorities caused the establishment to be removed to the opposite side of the Haven. Thus arose the modern town of Pembroke Dock; and from these modest beginnings the place has continued to increase, both in size and importance, down to the present day.

In spite of its remoteness from the manufacturing districts, whence most of the tools, materials, etc., have to be brought, the work is turned out in a style that would do credit to any establishment, by as steady, thrifty a set of men as is to be found in any Government yard. The workmen dwell in rows of neat cottages, forming a small town at the rear of the slipways. Though unpicturesque enough, these modest dwellings appear clean and sanitary, although unfortunately still lacking that prime necessity, a constant supply of pure water.

The adjacent hill is crowned by a heavily-armed redoubt, while many a vantage-point of the winding waterway is so strongly fortified that, should an enemy endeavour to force a passage, he would probably experience a *mauvais quart d'heure* in the warm welcome prepared for him.

From Pembroke a short run by train, and a ten minutes' walk through dull, workaday streets lands us at the dockyard gates. Before passing through, a constable politely relieves the visitors of such parlous *impedimenta* as fusees, lucifer matches and the like inflammables. Thence we are handed on to a stalwart sergeant, who without more ado pioneers us around the constructing sheds. Work is now in full swing, and the ring of riveters' hammers and clang of resonant metal combine, with a thousand other ear-splitting sounds, to swell an uproar fit to awaken the Seven Sleepers.

By dint of stentorian shouting, our *cicerone* explains the various details of construction ; now descanting on the special merits of a swift 'torpedo-catcher,' anon describing the internal economy of a half-completed gunboat. Meanwhile weird, Rembrandtesque effects of light and shade are seen on every side, as the men ply their heavy labour in the gloom of the iron-ribbed hull.

Thence we pass onward to a gigantic shed, lofty as a cathedral, with its forefoot planted in the sea. Here the rudimentary ribs of a huge ironclad swell upward from the keel-plate, resembling the skeleton of some antediluvian monster of the deep.

Farther on we come to long ranges of spacious workshops, crammed with machinery of the latest types propelled by engines both ancient and modern. By means of these, thick metal plates and beams are shaped and fashioned as easily as wood in a carpenter's shop. Here lies a massive bronze casting weighing many tons, destined to form the ram of H.M.S. *Renown;* yonder a metal plane shaves off golden spirals, much like the 'corkscrew' curls of other days, from a plate of solid brass. In another direction a strapping mechanic is bringing a steel plate to the requisite curve, by means of herculean blows from a heavy sledge.

Pass we now to the iron foundry, where a gang of workmen are about to draw the glowing metal from the furnace. The scintillating mass is hitched on to a movable crane, and borne away to be manipulated between a pair of massive metal rollers. After several successive squeezes, it emerges in the form of a huge armour plate.

Now, too, the Nasmyth hammer is much *en évidence*, its mighty strokes shaking the solid ground as we approach ; yet so docile is the monster that the engineer cracks a nut beneath it, to the no small astonishment of the visitors.

FROM UPTON CHAPEL.

Nor must we omit a peep at the wood-working shops, where the circular saw sings at its work the live-long day, shearing the roughest logs into comely planks with wonderful precision, while skilful hands fashion and frame the various parts required.

All these multifarious handicrafts, carried on in extensive and inflammable structures, necessitate an efficient fire-extinguishing apparatus. This is maintained in a separate building, and is kept in apple-pie order, ever ready to fight the flames in case of an outbreak of the devouring element.

*   *   *   *   *   *

Resuming our peregrinations 'in search of the picturesque,' we now bid farewell to the county-town of Pembroke. At Hobb's Point a grimy little steamboat, that years ago plied on the Thames, ferries the traveller across to the railway pontoon at New Milford, whence we entrain *en route* for Haverfordwest.

Rail and river keep company for a time through a pleasant, undulating country, with copsewood feathering down to the water's edge. Presently we pass close to Rosemarket, a primitive-looking village where, in the days of the Stuarts, dwelt a certain fair maid named Lucy Walters.

Here at the age of seventeen 'that browne, beautifull, bold but insipid creature,' as Evelyn calls her, was discovered by the gay Prince Charlie, who was so fascinated by the young lady's charms that he bore her away with him in his cavalcade.

LUCY WALTERS.

Lucy's grandfather it is said constructed a fine genealogical tree, in which that gay lady figures as 'married to King Charles y^e Seconde of England.'

The house where Lucy Walters' father lived has long since disappeared, the only relics of that period being probably the old stone pigeon-house east of the village, and the parish cockpit !

Our sketch of the famous beauty is copied from a contemporary portrait, brought from Dale Castle, whither the Walters family removed from their earlier home. It is now in the possession of a gentleman residing near Pembroke, who has kindly allowed us to make the accompanying copy.

The next station is Johnston, where we will break our journey and take a peep at the church, whose steeple we descry as the train approaches the station. The little structure stands, with a few cottages grouped around it, at a corner of the lanes ; and its gray, time-worn stones make a pretty picture amidst their setting of fresh green foliage.

At the western end of the church rises a small but ancient tower, with roof fast falling to decay. The lower part is solid, but towards the top it is pierced with a quartette of graceful, traceried windows,

of which three have been blocked up ; while the only bell the church could boast lies broken in two on the stone floor.

Small as it is, the church has shallow projecting bays, or chapels, after the manner of double transepts. Between them rises the chancel arch, devoid of features save a quaint, square-headed opening on either side, enclosing two small pointed arches.

The interior, with its two-decker pulpit, simple box-pews and ancient font, has a quiet, old-world look ; and the chancel, raised one

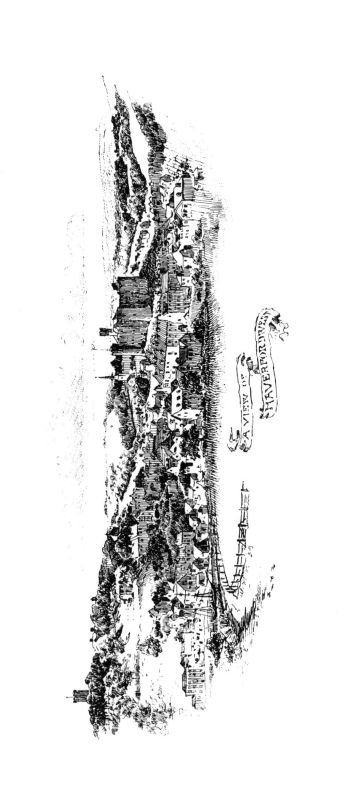

A VIEW OF HAVERFORDWEST

step only above the body of the church, contains a double sedilia, a small piscina and a few other early features.

Rumour hath it that the 'restorer,' save the mark! already lays his plans for the undoing of this interesting structure. However, as the attention of the Society for the Protection of Ancient Buildings has been given to the subject, we may hope that their praiseworthy efforts to maintain the ancient features of this church, in their un-restored simplicity, will eventually be crowned with success.

A long league's trudge still separates us from Haverfordwest; so we breast the easy slope of Drudgeman's Hill, and presently descend to Merlin's Bridge, spanning an affluent of the Cleddau. A scattered group of cottages that overlooks the stream bears some slight traces of the chapel that formerly stood here. A kind of Vanity Fair was formerly held in the vicinity, when the country folk foregathered at Cradock's Well, a wonder-working spring frequented by a hermit who had his cell at Haroldstone.

The Perrots of Haroldstone were great people in their time. Here dwelt the gallant Sir John Perrot, Lord Deputy of the Sister Isle in good Queen Bess's reign; also Sir Herbert of that ilk, the contemporary and friend of Addison, who is said to have been the original of that pink of courtesy, the incomparable Sir Roger de Coverley.

We now make a short *détour* to visit the ruins of Haverfordwest Priory, which stand in a meadow close beside the Cleddau. Though of considerable extent, there is not much to detain us here save a mass of crumbling arches and ivy-mantled walls, apparently of Early English date. This priory was established about the year 1200 by Robert de Haverford, first Lord of Haverfordwest, for the Order of Black Canons. It stands in one of those pleasant, riverside nooks that the monks of old so frequently selected.

The massive tower of St. Thomas's Church, crowning the brow of an adjacent hill, forms a conspicuous feature in our general view of the town. Though much modernized, this church contains one relic of the past that must on no account be overlooked.

Upon the pavement of the north aisle is preserved an ancient slab of limestone, whose battered surface is carved in low relief with a beautiful, foliated cross, terminating in trefoils; beside the cross is an object resembling a palm branch, and a closer inspection reveals, incised upon the edge of the stone, the legend: F RICARD LE PAUMER GIT ICI DEU DE SAALME EIT MERCI AMEN.

According to the verdict of the antiquaries, this curious monument records a certain brother Richard the Palmer, who, in days so remote as the time of Giraldus Cambrensis, journeyed as a pilgrim to Rome; or it may be joined as a recruit in the Crusade of Bishop Baldwin.

Up in the tower we discover a brace of fine old bells, the larger

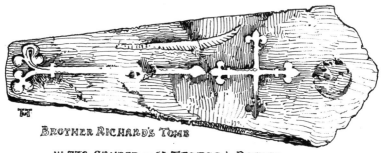

BROTHER RICHARD'S TOMB

IN THE CHURCH OF ST THOMAS À BECKET

HAVERFORDWEST.

one bearing the motto SANCTUS GABRIEL ORA PRO NOBIS; the smaller, or sanctus bell, GEVE THANKES TO GOD, T. W. 1585.

This church was formerly a possession of the Perrots of Harold-stone, until in Queen Elizabeth's reign the Crown became, as it has ever since remained, the patron of the living.

Let us glance back into the past as we stroll through the clean, bustling streets of the little Western metropolis.

From the earliest times Haverfordwest held a position second only in importance to that of Pembroke, as a bulwark of The Little England beyond Wales.

Its castle, built by Gilbert de Clare, first Earl of Pembroke, stood as a protection to the English settlement against the incursions of the hardy mountaineers, who had been driven back by the advancing immigrants upon the wild hill fastnesses of the interior.

The lofty walls of Gilbert's ruined castle, dominating the town that clusters around its feet, and the mediæval churches that rise

SAINT MARYS
HAVERFORDWEST.

amidst its steep, paved streets, recall the vanished *prestige* of Haverfordwest; while a characteristic vein of local dialect, which lingers yet despite of Board Schools, attests the foreign ancestry of some of the worthy townsfolk.

Curiously enough, Haverfordwest forms a county all to itself;

and is further distinguished by the fact that, alone amongst the towns of Great Britain, the place boasts a Lord-Lieutenant all its own, a privilege obtained from the Crown by a very early charter, when Pembrokeshire was a County Palatine.

The town formerly returned its own member to Parliament, but of late the representation has been merged in the districts of Pembroke, Tenby and Haverfordwest.

But it is time to look about us, so we now make our way to St. Mary's church, in the centre of the town.

Contrasted with the primitive structures we have seen in the country parishes, this is a noble church indeed, having been in large part constructed during the best period of Gothic architecture. The lofty nave is covered with a flat wooden ceiling, relieved by enriched bosses at the intersections of the beams, and upborne by handsome brackets against the walls. It is connected with the adjacent aisle by a series of richly-moulded arches, supported upon tall clustered pillars.

On the north side of the chancel stands a group of thirteenth-century pillars and arches of still more elaborate character, whose capitals are encrusted with a variety of grotesque figures intertwined amongst deeply-cut foliage.

Handsome traceried windows admit a flood of light into the chancel, whose walls display monuments and epitaphs of no little beauty and interest.

In a remote untended corner of the church lies the mutilated effigy of an ecclesiastic, whose sober livery, and wallet embellished with scallop-shells, mark him as a pilgrim who has crossed the seas to the shrine of St. James of Compostella, in Spain.

Passing out by the north porch, we observe a pair of tall, carved bench-ends, on one of which St. George is seen in combat with a triple-headed dragon. A sketch of this bench-end will be found at the head of Chapter XII.

After glancing at St. Martin's, the mother church of Haverfordwest, with its slender, crooked spire, we turn townwards again as dusk creeps on, and come to anchor at the Mariners Hotel. The old-fashioned hospitality of this comfortable inn is a welcome relief after a long day's tramp, so we cannot do better than make it our headquarters while exploring the surrounding country.

ARMS OF HAVERFORDWEST

17

CHAPTER VII.

TO ST. BRIDES, MARLOES AND THE DALE COUNTRY.

THE IRREGULAR island-girt peninsula lying between Milford Haven and St. Bride's Bay presents but few attractions for the ordinary tourist, to whom, indeed, this portion of Pembrokeshire is practically a *terra incognita.* Nevertheless, the locality has its own characteristic features, which the appreciative traveller will probably enjoy none the less for having to discover them for himself, unaided by the guide-books.

Availing ourselves of one of the numerous vehicles that ply during summer-time between Haverfordwest and the sea-coast, we escape a tedious tramp of some seven miles or more.

About half-way out our attention is called to a plain, rough stone close by the wayside. This is known as Hang-stone Davey, from the fact that a noted sheep-stealer of that ilk, halting to rest upon the stone with his ill-gotten booty slung around his neck, fell asleep and was strangled by the weight of his burden.

Presently the blue sea opens out ahead, and the lane makes a sudden turn over against a lonely country church. As we approach it, the little edifice presents such a curious medley of gables and turrets, as to tempt us to closer inspection.

Walton-West church has been carefully and wisely restored of recent years, and not before it was needed, for it is on record that in the 'good old times' two boys were kept at work on rainy Sundays, sweeping the water that flowed in at the porch into a pit formed in a disused pew. Eventually matters were brought to a climax by the snow falling through a rent in the roof, and lodging upon the bald head of an ancient worshipper! As usual, the tower, which appears never to have been completed, is the oldest remaining portion of the fabric;

WALTON WEST
CHURCH.

indeed, it has been considered as pre-Norman, a stone having, as we are informed, been found in the wall bearing the date A.D. 993. A small effigy, apparently of the Elizabethan period, built into the interior of the tower, is usually supposed to represent the patron saint of the church. Upon the north side of the chancel stands a well-proportioned chapel that formerly appertained to the family of Lort-Philipps.

WALWYNS CASTLE.

In an out-of-the-way spot, about a mile to the southward, lies the secluded hamlet of Walwyn's Castle. The distance is nearly doubled by the crooked lanes, but a pleasant field-path saves a longer *détour.*

SUMMER SHOWERS
LITTLE HAVEN.

From the brow of the hill we have three churches full in view, in diminishing perspective—Walwyn's Castle, down in the valley; Robeston, farther away; and Steynton, conspicuous upon a distant hill.

The church of Walwyn's Castle stands upon a gentle eminence that slopes to a hollow, wooded dingle overhanging a streamlet, whose waters meander away to a creek of the ubiquitous Haven.

The salient feature of the edifice is its tall, slender tower, and narrow stair-turret rising to the embattled roof. Upon the southern side the land falls away steeply, and the brow of the bank is scored with the grassy mounds of the ancient camp or castle, whence the place derives its curious name.

In an old black-letter chronicle of the sixteenth century it is recorded, ' In the Province of Wales which is callyd Roose, the sepulchre of Walwyne was found. He reigned in that parte of Britain which is callyd Walwythia. The Tombe was found in the days of William the Conqueror, King of England, upon the sea side, and contayned in length fourteen foote.'

A local variation of this time-honoured fable avers that Walwyn was buried on the site of the above-mentioned camp, and a sort of arched aperture, now fallen in and well-nigh obliterated, was formerly pointed out as the burial-place of this very 'lofty' hero.

· LITTLE HAVEN ·

Returning now to Walton, we descend a short but extremely steep bit of road to the village of Little Haven. A few fishermen's cottages,

LOW TIDE AT LITTLE HAVEN.

a homely inn and a handful of lodging-houses clambering up the rearward hill, form the sum total of this most diminutive of watering-places.

Seawards the hamlet is begirt by ruddy sandstone cliffs of moderate height, the rocky strata being twisted into the most curious contortions, and pierced with caverns and crannies frequented by bathers and picnic parties. The firm dry sands, exposed at low tide, afford a pleasant sea-side stroll to the more spacious shores of Broad Haven.

After calling a halt for a sketch of Little Haven, we up sticks and away, pursuing a south-westerly course by a road that climbs high above the rock-bound coast. Far below us lies a picturesque cove, with a rude flight of steps, hewn from the rock, leading to a landing-place used by the fisher-folk.

After passing Talbenny Church, we approach St. Brides, and obtain the pretty *coup d'œil* represented in the accompanying sketch: the church and old-fashioned rectory-house nestling under the lee of some wind-tossed trees, while Lord Kensington's fine residence of St. Brides Hill shows clearly out against the dark wood-lands that crest the western down. To the right is seen a glimpse of the tiny haven, famous in bygone times for its productive herring fishery. The little structure close beside the water occupies the site of an old fishermen's chapel, which, falling into ruins, was put to the degenerate uses of a salt-house. From that time forth, as the old story runs, the herrings deserted their accustomed haunts, and the fishing trade dwindled away:

> ' When St. Bride's Chapel a salt-house was made,
> St. Bride's lost the herring trade.'

The parish church is interesting, and has a bright, well-cared-for look that is pleasant to see. Upon the floor of a small north transept lie four sadly defaced effigies. The largest of these is reputed to represent St. Bride, the patron saint of the church, a contemporary of St. David and St. Patrick. According to tradition, St. Bride sailed over with certain devout women from Ireland, and established a nunnery here. A short distance south-east from the church rise the ivy-mantled ruins of some extensive buildings of unknown origin, overshadowed by dark trees and surrounded by lofty stone walls pierced with loopholes, while an arched gateway opens towards the west.

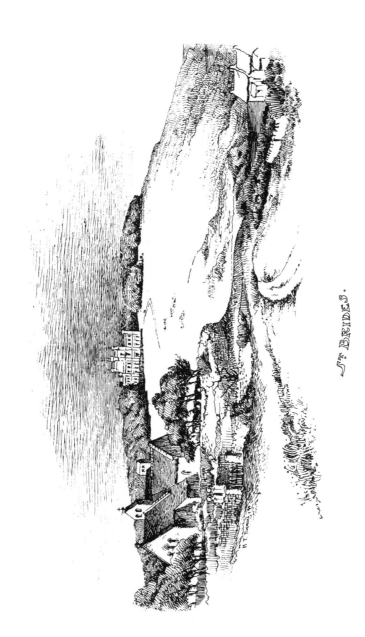

S^t· BRIDES·

Upon leaving St. Brides, we strike directly inland by the Dale road. This brings us in about a quarter of an hour to Orlandon, where the skeleton of a large old mansion rises grimly above a group of wayside cottages. In its palmy days Orlandon was the home of the Laugharnes, a family of some celebrity in their time, but now extinct in this locality.

According to a romantic story, the first member of this family who appeared in this district was shipwrecked and washed up more dead than alive on the seashore not far away. Here he was found by the

·ORLANDON·

daughter and heiress of Sir John de St. Brides, who caused him to be carried to her father's house, where he was hospitably entertained.

Laugharne, of course, was soon over head and ears in love with his fair deliverer, and the lady being in nowise backward in response to his suit, they married and founded a family whose descendants resided for generations at Orlandon.

Another mile brings us to Mullock Bridge, where a long causeway traverses a marshy backwater of the Haven. Anent this same bridge a quaint story is related concerning Sir Rhys ap Thomas of Carew. Having registered a vow before the King that Henry of Richmond

18

should not ascend the throne save *over his body*, the crafty knight fulfilled his word by crouching beneath the arch of Mullock bridge while Henry rode across it.

A glance at the map suggests a short *détour* to obtain a peep at Marloes. The sandy lane, meandering beside a streamlet, lands us right abreast of the church at the entrance to the village. The little edifice makes a pleasant picture, with a handful of low thatched cottages grouped around. Inside we find the small pointed chancel arch with projecting wings, characteristic of the churches in this locality.

There are some curious features here, notably an old bronze sanctus bell, and a modern baptistery sunk in a corner of the floor, to meet the predilections of the Welsh churchman, who does not apparently consider the ceremony of baptism complete unless he can 'goo throw the watter.'

MULLOCK
BRIDGE

Dwelling apart from the busier haunts of men, the good folk of this remote parish have kept pretty much to themselves, and have acquired the reputation of being a simple-minded, superstitious race—'Marloes gulls,' as the saying is. In order to save the long Saturday's tramp to Haverford market, a Marloes man hit upon the ingenious device of walking *half* the distance on Friday, then returning home he would complete the *rest of the walk* the next day !

In the 'good old times,' if tales be true, these Marloes people were notorious wreckers. On dark tempestuous nights they would hitch a lanthorn to a horse's tail, and drive the animal around the seaward cliffs ; then woe betide the hapless mariner who should set his course by this Fata Morgana ! There is a story of the parson who, when the

news of a wreck got abroad in church one Sunday morning, broke off
his discourse and exclaimed, 'Wait a moment, my brethren, and give
your pastor a fair start !'

Another mile of crooked, crankling lanes takes us to the brow of
the sea cliffs, whence we obtain a bird's-eye panorama of the broad
sweep of Marloes sands. Ruddy sandstone rocks pitched at a steep
angle encompass the bay, and peep grimly out from beneath the smooth,
firm sands. Gateholm rises close in shore, an island at low tide only ;
the broad mass of Skokholm stretches out to sea, while the horizon line

MARLOES

is broken by the lonely islet of Grassholm, a favourite haunt of sea birds,
and scene of a notorious 'massacre of the innocents' by a party of yachts-
men, some few years ago.

The frequent recurrence of these *holms* and other place-names of
Scandinavian origin, points unmistakeably to the presence of those old
sea rovers around the Pembrokeshire coast, in the days of 'auld langsyne.'

Making our way to the farm called Little Marloes, we push on
through heathy byways, approaching the coast again at West Dale Bay.
Now we catch a glimpse of Dale Castle, with the village of that ilk
nestling under the lee of a dark wood, and harvest-fields crowning the

sunny hillside, while a silvery stretch of the Haven lies in the background.

Dale Castle appears to have been a place of some importance from very early times, though of its history we have but meagre records. In the year 1293 Robertus de Vale granted a charter for a weekly market at his manor-house of Vale, and here Sir Rhys ap Thomas entertained his future King after his landing at Mill Bay upon the adjacent coast.

This village of Dale is still a comely-looking spot, where the pleasant country residences of the gentlefolk rub shoulders with a

· MARLOES SANDS ·

sprinkling of homely cottages; yet withal the village has a certain air about it as of a place that has known better days. For Dale, it seems, was once a flourishing seaport, the abode of substantial sea captains and well-to-do merchant traders; while, if tales be true, the village folk drove a flourishing business in the contraband goods run in by the 'free trade' fraternity. In those days good Welsh ale was brewed at Dale by a family bearing the singular name of Runawae, who exported it in large quantities to Liverpool: hence Dale Street in that city is said to derive its title from this place.

We approach the village by a footpath, and pass betwixt the castle and the church. The fuchsias, hydrangeas, myrtle and laurustinas that brighten this little God's acre tell of a genial climate ; yet some of the headstones bear grim records of shipwrecked mariners, who lost their lives upon the iron-bound coast that shelters this favoured spot. Dale Church has a tall, unrestored tower, and possesses a slender silver chalice inscribed with the words ' Poculum Ecclesiæ de Dale, 1577.' A sketch of this cup will be found at the head of the present chapter.

The lane now runs below the luxuriant groves of Dale Hill, and then skirts the shores of the sheltered inlet called Dale Road. ' Dale Rode,' says George Owen, ' is a goodlye Baye and a fayre rode of great receipte ; one of the best Rodes and Bayes of al Milforde and best defended from al windes, the East and South East excepted. In al

DALE CASTLE
AND MILFORD
HAVEN

this Rode there is good landing at al times.' Close beside the water stands a humble alehouse called the Brig, which bears evident traces of its smuggler patrons, being literally honeycombed with cellars and secret cupboards for the storage of their booty. Even now the walls still reek with moisture, from the salt stored away in inaccessible corners during those piping times when that commodity was worth a couple of guineas the hundredweight.

We now direct our steps towards St. Anne's Head, in order to visit Mill Bay, the traditional landing-place of Henry of Richmond. ' Here in Pembrokeshire,' says old George Owen, ' happened his landinge and first footeinge when he came to enoie the Crowne and to confounde the parricide and bluddie tyrante Ri : iii. Here founde he the heartes and hands first of all this lande readye to ayde and assist him.'　The saying goes that as he rushed up the steep bank at the head of his troop Henry, being scant of breath, exclaimed, 'This is Brunt!' a name that has clung to the neighbouring farm ever since.

After a flying visit to the lighthouses, we retrace our steps to Dale village, and, following a track around the head of the tideway, push on without a halt to Hoaton.　Here we find the huge old anchor shown in our sketch, and the question naturally arises, How did the anchor get there?　A vague tradition still lingers in the locality to the effect that, centuries ago, a big foreign man-o'-war was driven out of her course and

'THIS IS BRUNT.'

wrecked upon the shores of St. Bride's Bay.　Hence it has been con-jectured that this anchor may be a veritable relic of that 'wonderful great and strong' Spanish Armada, whose unwieldy galleons were cast ashore and dashed to pieces upon our western coasts, three hundred years ago.

Be that as it may, some years back the anchor, which had previously lain by the wayside, was dragged into the position where it now stands; the neighbours lending ready aid in response to offers of ale *ad lib*.　Fifty men with a team of horses were hard put-to to move it, for though much of the metal has rusted and flaked away, the shank is 20 feet long and nearly 30 inches thick, while the head of the anchor measures some 14 feet around, and the ring is large enough for a man to pass through. Truly that old Spanish galleon must have been a veritable Leviathan to require such an anchor as this !

From Hoaton we make our way across country to Haverfordwest, and traversing a district broken up into 'meane hills and dales,' we approach the town by way of the Portfield, and proceed to ' outspan ' at a certain snug hostelry not a hundred miles from St. Mary's broad steeple.

A RELIC OF THE
· SPANISH ARMADA ·

CHAPTER VIII.

'THESE HIGH wild hills and rough uneven ways, draw out our miles and make them wearisome.' Thus, league after league, the sorry team drags the battered old ramshackle coach up interminable ascents, or plunges in headlong career down rough, breakneck steeps, *en route* for that Ultima Thule of our wanderings, the ancient city of St. Davids. Sixteen miles and seventeen hills (so the story goes) lie between Haverfordwest and our destination. The route bears in a north-westerly direction, through monotonous country relieved by occasional glimpses of the strange, rugged rocks of Trefgarn, or a peep of more distant Precelly.

About half-way out rises the lofty isolated tower of Roch Castle, a border stronghold dominating the march-lands that for centuries formed the frontier of this 'Little England beyond Wales.' Built by Adam de Rupe in the thirteenth century, the tall, picturesque old tower forms a conspicuous object for miles around, while at its feet a group of whitewashed cottages cluster around the lowly parish church of St. Mary de Rupe.

Crossing the bridge that spans the Newgale Brook, we enter the ancient Welsh province of Dewisland. Presently our venerable quadrupeds are crawling at a snail's pace down a slanting hillside not quite so steep as a house-roof, with the village of Lower Solva squeezed into a crevice beneath our very feet.

The situation of this pretty hamlet recalls the Devonshire combe

that en-
folds with
such in-
imitable
grace the
village of
Clovelly.
Groups of
bowery
cottages
cluster
around

ROCH CASTLE.

the head of a landlocked haven,
which, small as it is, bears no in-
considerable traffic in coal, lime and
general produce from the Bristol
Channel ports, for distribution
throughout the western parts of
Pembrokeshire.

The rocky, weed-strewn shores
shelving up to low, grassy hills
overarched by the soft blue sky; a stranded coasting vessel, with
weather-stained canvas and rust-eaten anchor, beside a handful of rough
fishermen's cottages, present all that an artist could desire to compose
a charming picture.

From the crest of the hill near Upper Solva a wide view of the sea
opens out, with a brace of rocky islets off the coast; while far ahead
the high lands of Ramsey Isle, Carn Llidi and Pen Beri, raise their
graceful undulations above remote Octopitarum, and the wind-swept
sandhills that mark the site of legendary Menapia.

Coasting along through a rolling treeless country parallel with the
course of the Via Julia (the Roman road from Carmarthen), which
accompanies us henceforth to the end of our journey, we mount the
gentle ascent that leads to the time-honoured 'city,' of which, however,

19

little is seen until we are 'right there,' as our Transatlantic cousins say.

Dismounting at the Grove Hotel, we fare forth for our first view of time-honoured Tŷ Dewi, the city of St. Davids. Strolling leisurely along the quiet grass-grown 'street' of the village-city, we pause now and again to make way for a herd of cattle, or to watch a flock of geese, stubbing, with sinewy necks outstretched, in a damp and weed-grown corner. Presently the roadway

SOLVA HARBOUR.
FROM AN OLD PRINT.

widens out, and here stands an ancient stone cross, which, rising from a flight of time-worn steps, marks the central point of this most diminutive of cities.

Casting about for some clue to the whereabouts of St. Davids Cathedral, we soon espy a low, dark object that proves upon closer inspection to be the topmost story of the central tower. With this as guide, we traverse an old paved lane ycleped the Popples, *Anglicè* Pebbles, and passing beneath the tower gate—sole survivor of the four gate towers of the ancient city—enter the cathedral precincts. This point affords perhaps the most characteristic *coup d'œil* of the venerable edifice, set amidst that stern and sombre landscape with which its time-worn architecture so completely harmonizes.

Viewed from our present vantage-point St. Davids Cathedral appears

ST. DRUIDS CATHEDRAL

ensconced within the hollow of the vale, its topmost pinnacles scarce rising clear of the distant horizon. Grouped around the central mass of the cathedral stand the crumbling ruins of mediæval structures of scarcely inferior interest. Away to our left, beyond a grove of wind-swept trees, rise the arcaded walls of Gower's incomparable palace, while the slender tower of St. Mary's College peeps over the long cathedral roof.

The stone wall that encompasses the cathedral-close upon its eastern side terminates in the massive octagonal tower, with Gothic doorway and windows, seen in the adjoining sketch. This is flanked again by the old gateway through which we have just entered.

The Gate Tower,
St Davids.

We now descend the broad flight of steps that, from their number, have been dubbed the 'Thirty-nine Articles.' Passing through the great south porch our eyes are greeted by a beautiful Decorated doorway, the work of Bishop Gower, which is adorned with exquisitely-carved figures and foliage encrusting arch and pillar. Here enclosed amidst intersecting branches we discern quaintly sculptured representations of the Root of Jesse, the Crucifixion, St. David with his harp, and various other saintly personages; yonder the artist tells the history of Adam and the birth of Eve; while overhead presides the Holy Trinity, flanked by angels with swinging censers—a veritable gem of mediæval sculpture.

Proceeding onward we now enter the nave, whose rich yet massive

architecture forms a unique and enduring memorial of the first Norman
bishop, Peter de Leia. The general effect is of breadth rather than
height, the solid cylindrical pillars supporting semicircular arches of
unusual width, wrought with the varied and elaborate ornamentation of
the Transitional Norman period.

Above this rises a series of lofty arches enclosing both clerestory
and triforium—a rather unusual arrangement—while a singular appearance is produced by the upward slope of the floor, and the outward lean
of walls and nave pillars, the latter being the result of an earthquake
that occurred in the thirteenth century.

The roof which spans the broad nave is one of the most notable

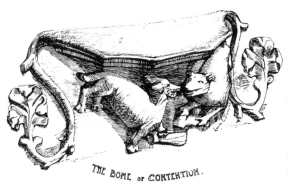

THE BONE of CONTENTION.

features of the cathe-
dral. It was built of
gray Irish oak about
the end of the fifteenth
century, and is a verit-
able masterpiece of con-
struction and design.
The sculptured foliage
of the capitals is worthy
of close examination,
and one of the nave
pillars bears a faded fresco, generally supposed to represent King
Henry IV. Beneath an adjacent arch reposes the effigy of Bishop
Morgan—a goodly figure habited in priestly robes that are admirably
rendered by the sculptor's chisel. The base of this monument is
enriched with an unusually fine Resurrection, carved in marble.

Fronting the full width of the nave, the beautiful Decorated rood
screen of Bishop Gower now claims our attention. This exquisite
structure is perhaps unrivalled in the picturesque variety of its several
parts, and the charming effects of light and shade that enhance the
mellow tones of its ancient stonework. Panelled buttresses divide the
screen into five bays, the middle compartment forming a wide archway
adorned with flowers and vine-leaves. To the left is the older portion,

subdivided by Gothic arches borne by detached pillars, with grotesque heads and figures clad in thirteenth-century armour. A narrow stair winds up to the ancient rood-loft above.

Turning to the southern side of the rood-screen, we are confronted by the rich and sumptuous fabric erected by Bishop Gower, a view of which forms the Frontispiece of the present volume. Yonder the noble founder sleeps his last sleep beneath a richly-groined canopy, whose traceried arches sparkle with cusps and crockets—a dignified, reposeful figure, worthy the Wykeham of the West, as Gower has been fitly styled. In memory of his greatest work Gower's tomb once bore the legend, ' Henricus Gower, Episcopalis Palatio Constructor.'

SEAFARING PILGRIMS.

After gazing our fill upon this beautiful structure, unquestion- ably the *chef d'œuvre* of the whole cathedral, we pass through the central archway be- neath a vaulted roof, whose stony ribs, dis- daining the customary support, spring clear of the circumjacent masonry. Here venerable tombs cluster beneath fretted ceilings that retain much of their ancient coloured fresco work, depicting figures, foliage, and fantastic forms which in nowise transgress the Scriptural commandment, for they bear little or no resemblance to any created thing.

We next enter the choir, which occupies the space beneath the central tower. Upon either hand extends a range of canopied stalls, with seats devoted to the use of the dean and chapter of the cathedral.

These old miserere seats were so ingeniously balanced that if an unwary brother chanced to nod over his breviary, he was quickly brought to his seven senses by the overturning of his treacherous perch.

The under-sides of these curious benches have been adorned by the craftsmen of that bygone time with the quaint conceits of their mediæval fancy. Here, for instance, a vigorously carved panel portrays in unmistakeable fashion the woebegone plight of two seafaring pilgrims, whom a pair of jolly monks are ferrying across the troubled waters of Ramsey Sound.

Yonder some subtle humorist has been at work, and given us his version of the priest under the guise of a fox administering the wafer to a goose of a layman; and it may be noticed that (after the olden custom) the priest reserves the wine flagon to himself. This forms the subject of our sketch at end of Chapter VIII. Two wolfish-looking dogs snarling over a bone may by some be thought to prove the antiquity of the familiar couplet,

> ' Taffy was a Welshman, Taffy was a thief,
> Taffy came to my house and stole a piece of beef.'

Then we have a couple of sturdy boat-builders, one of whom, having laid aside his adze, drains the contents of a capacious cup, while a mighty beaker stands ready to his hand.

THE BOATBUILDERS.

With such-like quaint original devices have those men of old encrusted the surface of these ancient stalls. So, having done justice to their curious details, we pass on through a *second* screen separating the chancel from the presbytery, an arrangement peculiar, we believe, to St. Davids Cathedral. This portion of the fabric was rebuilt with pointed arches after the fall of the central tower in 1220, and contains some extremely interesting features.

The place of honour in the centre of the presbytery is occupied by the tomb of Edmund Tudor, father of Henry VII., a massive table monument of Purbeck marble, enriched with shields and heraldic devices, and bearing the proud inscription : ' Under this Marble Shrine here enclos'd resteth the Bones of that noble Lord, Edmund Earl of Richmond, Father and Brother to Kings, the which departed out of this World in the Year of our Lord God a thousand four hundred fifty and six, the first Day of the Month of November, on whose Soul almighty Jesus have Mercy, Amen.'

Saint Davids Shrine

Upon the north side of the presbytery rises the stone structure that formed the base of St. David's Shrine. It is the work of Bishop Richard de Carew, and dates from the latter half of the thirteenth century. The three arches seen in our sketch were once adorned with figures representing St. David, St. Patrick and St. Denis, while the quatrefoil openings beneath were provided with small lockers to receive the offerings of devotees. In the presbytery we also notice a small circular piscina of very ancient date pierced with concentric rows of holes—a rare and curious feature.

After examining the handsome effigy of Bishop Anselm Le Gros, nephew of Earl William of Pembroke, with its laconic couplet—

' Petra Precor dic sic
Anselmus Episcopus jacet hic '

20

two fine recumbent figures of very ancient date arrest our attention, none other than those famous South Welsh princes, the Lord Rhys ap Gruffydd and his son, Rhys Grygg.

Higden, in his quaint ' Polychronicon,' breaks forth into unbounded panegyrics over the great Lord Rhys: ' O blysse of battayle !' he exclaims, ' Chylde of Chyvalry ! defence of Countrie ! worshyppe of Armes ! the noble dyadame of fayrnesse of Wales is now fallen, that is, Rees is dead. The Enemy is heere, for Rees is not heere ; now Wales helpeth not itself; Rees is dead and taken away, but hys noble Name is not dead, for it is always new in the wide Worlde. His Prowesse passeth hys manners ; hys Wytte passeth hys Prowesse ; hys fayre Speech passeth hys Wytte ; hys good Thews passeth hys fayre Speech !'

Not to prolong the subject *ad nauseam,* we will merely indicate as more particularly worthy of notice the tomb of Silvester Medicus ; a recumbent effigy *reputed* to be that of Giraldus Cambrensis, of Manorbere ; the massive shrine of St. Caradoc ; and two early Celtic crosses in the south transept, bearing the device $\overline{\overline{\wedge}}$ $\overline{\overline{\varphi}}$, with the legend PONTIFICIS ABRAHAM FILII.

We next glance into St. Thomas's Chapel, one of the oldest portions of the fabric, whose massive groined roof is adorned with sculptured bosses of unusual size. Here is a piscina enclosed within a group of pointed arches, whose lovely Early English enrichments form one of the daintiest features of the cathedral.

We now enter the beautiful chapel erected by Edward Vaughan, the last of the great building prelates of St. Davids. It boasts a handsome fan-vaulted ceiling, and a peculiar hagioscope fashioned like a cross within a circle.

Some curious details attract our notice as we wander amongst the unrestored chapels. In one of these, a trio of sculptured quadrupeds suggests the idea of the Trinity, while another contains the effigy of a knight in chain-mail, shorn of half its length by a clumsy buttress—a legacy from the days of churchwarden misrule.

Outside the Lady Chapel stood St. Mary's Well, which according to tradition arose at the prayer of St. David to supply the neighbouring monastery. Giraldus tells us that this accommodating spring would sometimes flow with wine, at other times with milk, and that it was the scene of many edifying miracles.

Sauntering around the mellow-tinted walls of the old cathedral, we notice the huge flying buttresses built against its northern side to strengthen the fabric. These rugged bastions, clothed in their luxuriant mantle of ivy, with the crumbling arches of the ruined cloisters hard by, group in a picturesque fashion beneath the central tower, whose broad front, bronzed by the rays of the declining sun, forms a rallying-point for a host of homing jackdaws.

A bowshot westward of the cathedral stand the beautiful ruins of the Bishop's Palace, rising from amidst the rich meadows beside the Allan River. Our route thither lies over the stony way called the Popples, the ancient approach to St. David's Shrine, and traverses the low-arched bridge that superseded the Llechllafar, or Speaking Stone, which in olden times spanned the stream at this point.

SYMBOL OF THE TRINITY
ST. DAVID'S.

Many a curious legend clung around this venerable stone, which Giraldus tells us was even in his time worn hollow by the feet of wayfarers. Tradition avers that Llechllafar was wont to cry out in remonstrance if a corpse was carried across it; and Merlin is said to have foretold that an English king, returning from the conquest of Ireland, was to meet his death upon this spot. So when Henry II. chanced this way, a disappointed suppliant endeavoured to foist this sinister prediction upon him; but the King, having made a suitable oration to the stone, passed over it unharmed to make his orisons before the Shrine of St. David.

Turning from the scene of these miraculous events, we pass a group of lowly cottages and enter the ruined gateway of the palace. Across a stretch of greensward, close-cropped by flocks of sheep, rise the ruined walls of Bishop Gower's lordly dwelling; the open-arched parapets casting a dappled shade athwart the grass-grown courtyard.

Built in the Decorated style that prevailed throughout the fourteenth

BISHOP GOWER'S PALACE
Sᵗ DAVIDS.

century, this interesting structure extends around a quadrangle, of which two sides remain in fair preservation, the others being either much in ruins, or entirely razed to the ground. Everything here speaks of peace and bygone hospitality. A wide ogee archway adorned with sculptured niches gives access to the banqueting-hall, an apartment of noble proportions adorned with an exquisite rose window still in good pre-

THE PALACE
ST DAVIDS
FROM THE MEADOWS.

servation. Near at hand rises the chapel, with its picturesque bell-turret and pointed windows ; while over all runs a pretty open arcade, borne upon huge corbels embellished with grotesque heads and strange fantastic monsters. A pleasant variety has been obtained by arranging the stonework above the arches in a kind of diaper pattern, as may be seen in the accompanying sketch taken from the meadows, whence the rose window forms a very charming feature. With the lapse of time these venerable ruins have mellowed into all sorts of harmonious hues, where golden lichens, valerian and climbing plants innumerable, have run riot over the rough purple sandstone.

From the ford across the little stream beneath the palace walls, a charming view is obtained of the ancient bridge and its rough, ivy-clad abutments, backed by the massive front of the cathedral and the picturesque tower and arches of St. Mary's College.

Built by Bishop Adam Houghton towards the close of the fourteenth century, the college chapel, with its vast Perpendicular windows, must in former times have presented an imposing appearance. Here the founder lay at rest under a sumptuous canopy, of which, however, not a vestige now remains. Beneath the chapel is a low groined crypt, but the various collegiate offices which lay to the north have long since been swept away; while the crumbling arcades of the cloisters serve nowadays to shelter the benches of the masons employed in repairing the cathedral.

St. Non's Chapel, the reputed birthplace of St. David, stands in an open meadow overlooking the sea, about a mile outside the city. It is a mere tumbled mass of rude cyclopean masonry, and has no features worthy of note save a simple cross enclosed within a circle, engraved upon an upright slab of stone. An ancient well dedicated to St. Non, the mother of St. David, occupies a corner of the same field.

Some quaint traditions hang around the old chapel called Capel Stinian, whose scanty ruins overlook Ramsey Sound. St. Justinian, the patron saint, was treacherously slain by his own followers on Ramsey Island, whereupon the holy man arose, walked across the straits, and was buried where his chapel now stands. The assassins, having been smitten with leprosy, were banished to Gwahan Garreg, the Lepers' Rock. The story runs that the Puritans stole away the chapel bells, which were famed for their musical sound; but a great storm arising, the vessel in which they endeavoured to escape with their booty was overwhelmed, and the bells cast into the sea. So on stormy nights when the deep, strong tide is troubling the waters, the dwellers near Ramsey Sound still hear the chimes of those long-lost bells, above all the strife of the elements.

Across the straits rises the broad bulk of Ramsey Island: smooth and tame enough on this side, but presenting to the western ocean a grim array of tall inaccessible cliffs and gloomy caverns, the haunt of seals and sea-fowl innumerable. Farther out to sea lies the group of rocky islets known as the Bishop and his Clerks, 'who,' as George Owen has it, 'are not withoute some small Quiristers who shewe not themselves but at Spring Tydes and calme seas. The Bishop and these his Clerkes preache deadlie doctrine to their winter audience, such poore seafaring men as are forcyd thether by Tempest; onelie in one thinge are they to be commended ; they keep residence better than the canons of that see are wont to doo.'

Setting our course for the seagirt promontory of St. Davids Head, we direct our steps towards the curious-looking hill called Carn Llidi. The bold peak of this monticle rises straight before us as we trudge across the sandy burrows, which, in the course of ages, have invaded the site of Roman Menapia, the elder sister of St. Davids.

Thenceforward ensues an exhilarating stretch across the open boulder-strewn headland. Overhead the sun shines bright and warm, light fleecy clouds drift landward under a bracing sea-breeze, casting their purple shadows athwart the azure plain of ocean, which breaks in white foam upon the 'grisly, fiendy Rockys blake' that fringe the broad sweep of Whitesand Bay.

We now push on to the outermost crags of the headland. Stretching seawards like a long, crooked finger, this remote peninsula forms the most westerly landfall of Pembrokeshire, and the southernmost horn of that great Welsh gulf known as Cardigan Bay. Making our way over rough, rocky ground, we pass a huge half-fallen cromlech ; and, as the headland narrows, a crumbling rampart flanked by a half-obliterated fosse appears to bar all further progress. This ancient structure, called Clawdd y Millwyr, or the Warriors' Dyke, is constructed of smallish granite stones, compacted with soil and turf ; it runs in a slightly-curved line, which is convex upon the landward face, from sea to sea across the narrow peninsula.

Just within the shelter of the bank, upon a stretch of comparatively level greensward, lies one of those *cityau*, or groups of hut-circles, occasionally to be met with throughout Wales. Six at least of these primitive dwellings are here discernible, all within a few feet of one another, and each of considerable size ; many of the stones have sharp, square edges, and some appear to have been rudely shaped to the requisite curve of the circle.

Tradition itself is dumb regarding the origin of these mysterious structures ; but there can be little doubt they were erected at a very remote period.

Once again under way, we shape our course for the rocky peak of
Carn Llidi. Although barely 600 feet in height, this isolated monticle
is in its upper parts abrupt and precipitous. At first our path leads
away up the ferny slope to a sort of saddle-backed ridge, over whose
bare jagged ledges we clamber onwards until a short, sharp pull up a
kind of stony *couloir* lands us upon the topmost crag.

Here we seem to have mounted (like Jack on his Beanstalk) into
a new and undiscovered world, for this isolated perch affords a bird's-eye

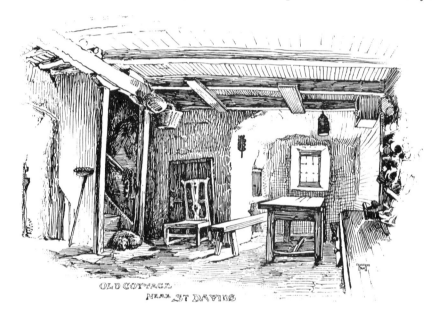

OLD COTTAGE
NEAR ST DAVIDS

view over land and sea that rolls away to the distant horizon. Far
beyond the broad expanse of Cardigan Bay the highlands of Snowdonia
loom faint but clear ; a wrinkled, treeless country, chequered by countless fields and dotted with white farm-houses, trends away league upon
league to the foot-hills of Precelly, and the smoke-begirt heights of
Glamorgan. Roch Castle, upon its lonely hillock, looks out across a
silver stretch of St. Bride's Bay to the islands of Ramsey and Skomer.
The village-city is hidden by an intervening rise, but its situation is

marked by the conspicuous windmill; and westwards St. Davids Head thrusts out like a crooked finger into the open sunlit ocean.

Descending the hill, we work our way along winding sandy lanes, and return to St. Davids by the coast road coming from Fishguard. At an out-of-the-way place called Gwryd-Bach we stumble across a curious old farmstead, and being invited to enter, we proceed to make ourselves at home in a large low chamber, half living-room, half kitchen. At one end of this picturesque apartment is a low-browed, vaulted recess, pierced with a deep-set window, while upon the rough flagged floor beneath stands a mighty oak table of extremely primitive build. The ample dresser beside the wall displays such an array of curious old painted plates, and mugs of antiquated pattern, as might make a connoisseur's fingers itch. One retired corner is partitioned off as a kind of homely parlour; on another side a rough open stairway gives access to the garret, while old guns, lanthorns, baskets and such-like articles of a rustic *ménage*, garnish every available corner of walls and open-rafted ceiling.

We return to St. Davids by way of Dowrog Common, the 'Pilgrims' land' of earlier days, with its huge upright *maenhir*, called St. David's Stone. Before turning in for the night we overhaul Ordnance maps and guide-book, in view of an early start upon the morrow in search of 'fresh woods and pastures new.'

THE PRIEST & THE LAYMAN.

CHAPTER IX.

TO FISHGUARD, NEWPORT, GOODWIC AND PENCAER.

 FULL FIVE tedious leagues of monotonous cross-country road lie before us to-day, as we leave St. Davids city northward bound for Fishguard. A sturdy pedestrian may strike out a more interesting route by following the coast road — the ancient Fordd Fleming—and diverging at convenient points to explore the grand cliff scenery below Pen-beri, and the microscopic havens of Trevine and Abercastell. At Longhouse, close to the latter place, stands a remarkably fine cromlech, inferior only to its more famous rival at Pentre Evan, near Newport.

About half-way along the main road we cross a country lane that follows the course of the old Fleming's Way; and half a mile farther  on our attention is called to an object not unlike a milestone, upon which is rudely traced a cross within a circle: the irregular disc being about a foot in diameter. This is known as Mesur-y-Dorth—the Measure of the Loaf—from a tradition that St. David caused these figures to be made in order to regulate the size of the loaf of bread in times of scarcity.

Presently we approach the village of Jordanston; and here it behoves the belated traveller to 'keep his weather eye open,' for if tales be true, the ghost of a headless horseman that haunts this locality may be expected to put in an appearance.

A couple of miles or so to the northward rises the parish church of Mathry, conspicuous upon its high hill-top. This church of the Holy Martyrs once had a lofty steeple, that served as a useful guide to mariners until blown down one stormy night, many a year ago. Mathry was a place of some local importance in olden times, receiving a patent for a market and fair from Edward III., while the greater tithes of this extensive parish sufficed to endow the 'golden prebend' of St. Davids Cathedral.

As we near our destination, the rugged hills of Pencaer rise picturesquely beyond the sands of Goodwic, while Dinas head rears its bold front above Cardigan Bay, with the delicate outline of the Carnarvonshire mountains serrating the distant horizon.

The town of Fishguard hangs, as it were, upon the slope of a precipitous hill overlooking the vale of the Gwaen, which here, as George Owen puts it, 'falleth into the sea, making a faire Haven and goode Harborow for shipps and Barks.' Its waterside suburb of Abergwaen, approached by one of the steepest bits of coach road in the Principality, is mainly frequented by fisher-folk and seafaring men engaged in the coasting trade.

Encompassed by sheltering uplands, the narrow vale of the Gwaen has a singularly mild and equable climate, which fosters a wealth of luxuriant vegetation. In the course of a stroll through the beautiful grounds of Glyn-y-Mel, we notice the eucalyptus and bamboo evidently making themselves quite at home in this sunny nook, while heliotrope and dracæna, camellia and laurestinus flourish out-of-doors the winter through.

Usually the most easy-going of Sleepy Hollows, Fishguard town awoke one fine morning towards the close of the last century to find itself become suddenly famous. On February 21, 1797, three French frigates were sighted off the Pembrokeshire coast bearing up towards Fishguard Bay, where they presently came to anchor near Carreg Gwastad Point.

During the ensuing night the enemy came ashore to the number of about 1,500 men, regular troops and gaol-birds, under the leadership of one Tate, a renegade Irish-American. Tate, with the chief of his satellites, established himself at the neighbouring farmhouse of Trehowel, while the main body of the 'invaders' encamped atop of an isolated hill overlooking the village of Llanwnda. Thence the Frenchmen dispersed about the country-side, scaring the inhabitants out of their wits, and rummaging the farmhouses in search of potheen and plunder.

In one of these exploits a drunken fellow entered a cottage at Brestgarn, where a 'grandfather' clock happened to be standing in a corner. Dismayed by the sounds issuing from the mysterious object, the simpleton fired his gun at a venture, concluding the devil must be

lurking within. This clock is still to be seen at Brestgarn, with the bullet-hole through the panel as may be noticed in our sketch.

Meanwhile the authorities bestirred themselves. Under the command of Lord Cawdor, the Fishguard Fencibles and Castle Martin Yeomanry marched out to Goodwic Sands, where the enemy, finding the game was up, laid down their arms and surrendered *à discrétion*. Thus these doughty regiments achieved the unique distinction of facing a foreign foe on the soil of Britain itself. It is said that the goodwives of Pembrokeshire, arrayed in their red woollen 'whittles,' countermarched and deployed around a neighbouring hill, thus leading the invaders to suppose that a regiment of gallant redcoats was preparing to oppose their advance.

Clock at Brestgarn.

The French prisoners were subsequently lodged in durance vile at a place near Pembroke, whence some of them effected their escape in Lord Cawdor's yacht, with the connivance of two Pembroke lasses— the old story of *cherchez la femme* once more. One of the French vessels having been afterwards captured was re-christened the *Fisguard*, a name that has only recently disappeared from the files of the Navy List. Incredible as it may seem in these days, the news of this famous event took a whole week to travel to the Metropolis, and it is said that the anniversary of the French landing is still held in remembrance amongst the old folk in the locality.

It is a pleasant stroll from Fishguard to the scene of these historic events. Our way lies past the church, where, in a corner of the grave-yard, we notice a curiously-incised stone cross. The lane now winds downhill, and we soon find ourselves pacing the smooth firm expanse of Goodwic Sands, with the hamlet of that ilk clinging to a wooded hillside before us.

Goodwic is picturesquely situated, overlooking a tiny haven and pier in an elbow of the rock close under the hill. Its genial climate and

Lanwnda Church

safe bathing shore make the place deservedly popular, and cause the handful of lodging-houses to fill up rapidly during ' the season.'

Pushing on again, we now enter the district of Pencaer, and, guided by the trusty Ordnance sheet, thread our way through narrow crooked lanes, rounding the base of Carn Wnda, where the Frenchmen pitched their camp, and passing on to the little out-of-the-way village of Llanwnda.

The church stands in an isolated position overlooking a piece of rough ground that does duty as village ' green,' a place scattered over with gray tumbled stones that seem to group themselves into the lines of rude hut-circles. Two or three low thatched cottages, that might pass for Irish cabins, appear to have been 'dumped' down haphazard, and look old enough to have seen Giraldus Cambrensis when he held the benefice here.

Built in a strong, simple manner well-suited to its exposed situation, Llanwnda Church has some characteristic features. Above the western gable rises a low double bell-cot, while a similar but smaller erection for the sanctus bell divides nave from chancel roof. As we enter the low-browed porch, we espy a cross of archaic type carved upon a stone slab in the outer wall; and two similar crosses are to be seen upon the exterior of the chancel gable.

· THE CHALICE AT LLANWNDA ·

The nave retains its dark, oaken timbered roof, having a rudely carved head upon the eastern side of one of its ancient beams. The openings to the rood-loft are now blocked up, but at the time of the French incursion these apertures afforded a hiding-place to a servant-maid and child, who peeped out in trepidation whilst a gang of ruffians played havoc in the sacred edifice, setting fire to everything inflammable they could lay hands upon.

After some little persuasion Mary Reece, the sprightly nonagenarian care-taker, is prevailed upon to produce the communion chalice for our inspection. This little vessel has a history of its own, having been stolen by a Frenchman, who endeavoured to dispose of it at Carmarthen, trying to pass off the word Llanwnda engraved upon the cup as La Vendée, a name of France. The chalice, which is much cracked and dented from the rough handling it has undergone, bears upon the exterior the inscription : POCULUM ECLESIE DE LLANWNDA.

Pushing on across country, we win our way after half an hour's rough scrambling to Carreg Gwastad Point, a low, rocky, furze-clad headland sloping down to a secluded creek, where the would-be French invaders effected a landing.

A more out-of-the-way spot, or one more suited to embark on such an enterprise, they could not well have chosen. The wild and little-frequented coastline of Pencaer stretches away on either hand with scarce a vestige of a landing-place; while the scattered peasant-folk, dwelling in isolated cottages and lone farmhouses, could offer but an ineffectual resistance to the enemy.

We now extend our route to Trehowel, a large, rambling old farmstead shaded by trees, where the French commander took up his unwelcome billet. Thence we strike up the slope of Garn-vawr to the huge British camp that crowns the summit, a wide prospect over land and sea rewarding our exertions. Following the crest of the ridge, we enjoy a breezy tramp across country, sundry fallen cromlechs and such-like relics lending an old-world interest to the locality.

Anent the country of Pencaer there is a venerable tradition which runs somewhat to the following effect: 'Once upon a time' there was a town in Pencaer called Trêf Cwlhwc, or Cwlhwc's Town. This Cwlhwc appears to have been a sort of Celtic Hercules, who roamed about his native country in search of adventures. When grown to man's estate, Cwlhwc began to entertain ideas of marrying and settling down; whereupon he was informed by an oracle that no maid save the fair Olwen might become his wife. Nothing daunted, the giant set forth in quest of his future bride, and after searching for a year and a day found the beautiful Olwen seated alone in her bower.

'She was arrayed,' says the old Welsh Mabinogion, 'in a vesture of flame-coloured silk, a wreath of ruddy gold was about the damsel's neck, set with pearl and coral. More yellow was her head than the blossoms of the broom; her skin was whiter than the foam of the wave; her fingers fairer than the opening buds of the water-lily, amid the small ripplings of the fountain of the waters. No brighter eyes than hers were seen; whiter was her bosom than the breast of the swan, more red her cheeks than the rose of the mountain. Whoever saw her was filled with love, and in her every footstep four white trefoils sprang wherever she trod, and therefore she was named Olwen.'

The Royal Oak inn at Fishguard (see head of present chapter) formed the British headquarters in the affair of '97. Trundling out of the town by the Newport coach, we skirt the slopes of Carn Enoch, across whose western flank extend the lines of prehistoric *maenhirs* known as Parc y Marw, the Field of the Dead. Away to our left rises the big bluff headland that shelters the village of Dinas, whose pretty cottages peep out from amidst bowery orchards upon a little secluded cove. A new church has supplanted the old one, of which the western wall alone remains, all else having been swept away by inroads of the sea.

Our route now leads around the rocky shores of Newport Bay, the rough country lane affording some refreshing glimpses of narrow inlets, with woodlands feathering down to the water's edge. As we advance, the dark brow of Carn Englyn swings into view, with the houses of Newport clustering about its lower slopes. Arrived at that pleasant country town we beat up quarters for the night, intending to make it our head centre while exploring that portion of the shire stretching from the foot-hills of Precelly to the shores of Cardigan Bay.

A DERELICT.

CHAPTER X.

WE NOW enter upon that portion of Pembrokeshire distinguished from earliest times by the name of Kemaes, a district that was constituted a Lordship Marcher by the Norman invaders of Wales.

The first conqueror established himself in a strong castle at Newport, which formed the *Caput Baroniæ*, or chief place of the district. Here the Lord Marcher of Kemaes held his court in almost regal state, exercising practically unlimited control over the lives and property of his newly-conquered vassals. After the manner of the times, the Lord of Kemaes was empowered to deal summarily with felons, for whom a gaol was provided within the castle precincts, where a gibbet stood on a mound called by the natives Cnwc y Crogwydd, or Gallows Tump.

Amongst the privileges peculiar to this lordship was the patronage of the British Bards, and the disposal of a much-prized silver harp, which was treasured in the ancient abbey of St. Dogmaels, near Cardigan.

Standing upon a gentle declivity overlooking the town and bay, Newport Castle owes its origin to William, son of Martin de Turribus, the conqueror of Kemaes. The date of its erection appears to have been about the close of the eleventh century, but the castle was probably altered or enlarged by subsequent rulers.

In Queen Elizabeth's time that curious antiquary George Owen paid a visit to Newport Castle, in which he noticed 'faire and lardg

22

Roomes'; moreover, he tells us the place 'was moatid with a clear Springe of swete running Water, out of whiche, after it had pleasured the Eye in that capacitie, by a sluice it was let foorth to drive the myll, called the Castle myll, adjoininge the sayd moate.'

Of this lordly structure the entrance archway, flanked by two noble crenellated towers, are the best preserved features; but extensive ruins of walls and circular bastions, encompassed by the half-obliterated moat, may still be traced upon its western side.

Nestling beneath the castle, on the outskirts of the town, stands the handsome parish church of St. Byrnach. The original edifice is said to have been erected by the builder of Newport Castle, but the present Decorated structure has superseded a building of later date that was the very epitome of ugliness. Within the church stands a very early font, probably the original one of Norman times. Of the finely wrought and gilded rood-screen it is said once to have possessed, not a vestige has been preserved.

St. Byrnach, the patron saint of Newport Church, was an Irishman by birth, and a contemporary of St. David. He appears to have been held in high esteem throughout all this district, where many of the parish churches are dedicated to his name. This holy man is supposed to have led the life of a hermit, dividing his time between Buarth Byrnach, or Byrnach's Fold, on the singular mountain called Carnedd Meibion Owen, and the rocky recesses of Carn Englyn, the Angel's Peak, above Newport town, a hill that derives its name from a tradition that St. Byrnach was nourished by angels during his lonely sojourn there.

But *revenons à nos moutons.* Newport was anciently a borough town, having obtained its charter of incorporation as early as A.D. 1215. The town also received the grant of a market from Sir Nicholas FitzMartin, Lord of Kemaes, in the year 1278. This ancient document is still extant. Henceforth Newport continued to grow and prosper, and in the sixteenth century carried on extensive woollen manufactures. Upon the outbreak of the 'sweating sickness,' the place suffered severely; its market was discontinued, and many of the inhabitants fled to the more salubrious air of Fishguard.

Though its privileges have been much curtailed in modern times, the town has still n~minally~ a municipal body, though the latter has neither revenues to dispose of, nor functions to perform. Of recent years, however, Newport has shown signs of re-awakening prosperity ; and when the long-talked-of railway line becomes a *fait accompli*, this pleasant little market town will doubtless enter upon a new lease of life and activity.

At Parrog, where the Nevern stream embouches upon Newport Bay, we find a watering-place in its infancy. Parrog is an attractive spot in a quiet sort of way, and draws a fair sprinkling of holiday-makers from up the country during the long days of summer. A few comfortable if unpretentious lodging-houses offer decent accommodation, and cater in a manner that leaves little to be desired where criticism is disarmed by lusty appetites, bred of long hours spent in the brine-laden air. The neighbourhood, too, is pleasantly diversified, and contains many secluded nooks affording charming rural rambles.

But to return to Newport. At the farther end of the town, after passing the Llwyngwair Arms, we turn down a lane in the direction of the river, and in a couple of hundred paces descry a cromlech standing amidst an adjacent meadow. Though smaller than many others in the county, this cromlech is in a good state of preservation, and, as may be seen in the sketch at the end of the chapter, possesses an uncommonly massive capstone.

Retracing our steps to the highroad, we then jog pleasantly along beneath the welcome shade of an avenue of trees. Just beyond Pont Clydach, we enter the grounds of Llwyngwair by a meadow path that winds amidst delightful groves, where oak, beech, and ash shelter a wealth of tangled undergrowth.

Crossing a couple of fat grazing meadows, decked with hemlock and fragrant meadowsweet, we find ourselves on the brink of the Nevern Brook, a genuine Welsh streamlet that rushes briskly onward in deep brown pools and broken, shingly reaches—

> ' With here and there a lusty trout;
> And here and there a grayling.'

This Nevern stream rises far away on the slopes of Fryn-y-Fawr, whence, after pursuing a picturesque course below Pencelly forest, it finds its way by many a 'crankling nook' to Nevern, where it is spanned by a graceful old stone bridge, whose buttresses are shrouded in luxuriant ivy.

Over this same bridge we presently take our way, passing the lowly village school-house, whence the sing-song iteration of young voices salutes our ears through wide-open windows. In another minute we find ourselves at the churchyard wicket, where we pause awhile to look about us and take our bearings.

The village of Nevern is situated in the richly-wooded glen of the Dûad, or Nevern Brook, and is surrounded by some of the most charming scenery in the county. The luxuriant groves of Llwyngwair afford shelter from the strong sea winds, while the purple shoulders of Precelly sweep upward in graceful folds to the lofty southern horizon. The picturesque peak of Carn Englyn forms a prominent feature in the landscape; and, separated from it by the deep, narrow vale of the Clydach, rises Carnedd Meibion Owen, a rocky monticle that reminds one strongly of the Dartmoor Tors.

Time was, 'tis said, when this village of Nevern took precedence of its rival neighbour Newport. In those early days Nevern was a borough town, having its own portreeve with courts of government, and eighteen 'burgages' to manage its affairs. Above the townlet rose the protecting walls of Llanhyvor Castle, a fortalice long regarded, so to speak, as a precious gem in the diadem of every South Wallian prince. A steep grassy knoll alone marks the site where this important castle stood.

But it is time to look at Nevern Church. Dedicated to St. Byrnach, this ancient structure presents, with its gray walls peeping amidst masses of dark foliage, a picturesque and venerable appearance. The western tower, though of no great height, is of vast breadth and substance, extending to the full width of the church, and having a projecting stair-turret upon its northern side. In this tower hangs a peal of six very musical bells.

Approaching the south porch, we pass beneath a dense avenue of ancient yews, which even at noontide cast a gloomy shade around. Though lacking aisles, the church has shallow transepts, that on the north being called the Glasdwr Chapel, while the south transept is

TRE-WERN CHAPEL & BYRHACKS CROSS NEVERN.

appropriated to the use of Trewern, an old mansion in the vicinity. This Trewern Chapel has a solidly groined stone ceiling and elegantly proportioned windows, with a projecting turret for the stairway, leading to an upper chamber, as depicted in the adjoining sketch.

Upon either side the chancel is a sort of shallow bay, lighted by a narrow pointed window, a characteristic feature of Pembrokeshire churches. The sacred edifice is provided with a pair of silver chalices dated respectively 1696 and 1733, the gifts of former parishioners.

Near the south-east angle of the Trewern Chapel rises the ancient Celtic cross that figures conspicuously in our sketch. This curious monument goes by the name of St. Byrnach's Stone. It stands upwards of 10 feet in height, and is overlaid with the interlacing ornament peculiar to these structures. So boldly and deeply are the patterns incised, as to be little the worse for ten centuries of wind and weather, the hoary lichens that cling to the rugged surface of the monolith serving but to enhance its venerable aspect.

Anent this ancient stone, there is a quaint tradition which tells how, in olden times, the cuckoo was wont to first sound his note in this locality on the day of the patron saint, April 7.

'I might well here omit,' says George Owen, 'an old report as yet fresh of this odious bird, that in the old world the parish priest of this church would not begin Mass until the bird—called the citizen's ambassador—had first appeared, and began her note on a stone called St. Byrnach's Stone, being curiously wrought with sundry sort of knots, standing upright in the churchyard of this parish; and one year staying very long, and the priest and the people expecting her accustomed coming (for I account this bird of the feminine gender), came at last, lighting on the said stone—her accustomed preaching-place—and being scarce able once to sound the note, presently fell dead.'

It is somewhat reassuring to be told by the same authority that 'this vulgar tale, although it concerns in some sort church matters, you may either believe or not without peril of damnation.'

Quitting the pleasant precincts of the church, we pursue a crooked lane that skirts the green mounds of the 'castell,' and, turning thence past a solitary thatched cottage, make our way along a hollow tree-shaded pathway. Keeping a sharp look-out upon every side, we presently espy the object of our search, the form of a cross, half obliter-ated by ivy sprays and tufts of rushy grass, being seen rudely graven upon the high sandstone bank by the lane side ; while a sort of hollow kneeling-place can be distinguished in the rock at the bottom of the cross.

For we are now upon the line of an ancient pilgrims' way, whose course is marked by well-worn tracks in the soft red sandy rock ; and this solitary cross calls up visions of the mediæval wayfarer pausing upon his journey to St. David's Shrine, to invoke before Croes Byrnach the benediction of that influential saint. We are at some pains (owing to the exuberant undergrowth) to obtain a sketch of this interesting object, for, so far as we are aware, no other cross like this is to be found throughout the length and breadth of Wales.

In an out - of - the - way locality about two miles north of Nevern stands a farmhouse called Trellyfan, *anglicè* Toadstown. The origin of this singular name is explained by the following story, narrated by no less an authority than the famous Giraldus Cambrensis.

One day in the course of his travels Giraldus fell in with an exceedingly tall young man, who, owing to the length of his limbs, was known as Sitsyllt of the Long Legs. The career of this ill-starred individual was cut short in a strange and tragic manner, the unhappy Sitsyllt being worried to death by *toads*, in spite of the fact that his friends had very considerately hung him up in a sack, to save him from the molestations of these malignant reptiles !

As a memento of this incident, the marble effigy of a toad was built into a chimney-piece at Trellyfan, where it was treasured for many generations.   The toad was afterwards cut away and removed from its place in the farmhouse, but eventually came into the possession of its present owner, a resident at Haverfordwest, by whose courtesy we are enabled to give a sketch of this venerable relic.   The toad in question is carved in a dark-green veined marble, about as large as the palm of a woman's hand, and is reputed to be the work of an Italian artist.

Retracing our steps to Nevern, we call a halt at the Trewern Arms, a modest hostelry so near the stream that its waters play a pleasant accompaniment during the course of our homely meal.   Then, with energies recruited, we plunge into a shadowy woodland path that leads to Pont-y-Baldwyn, a bridge that spans the rippling stream at a point where, according to tradition, Archbishop Baldwyn preached the crusade in company with Giraldus Cambrensis.

THE TOAD OF TRELLYFAN.

From Pont-y-Baldwyn we follow a farm road that leads us to Hênllys, a place memorable in Pembrokeshire annals as the birthplace of that industrious chronicler and local antiquary, George Owen of Hênllys.   Of his curious and fascinating work entitled ' The Description of Penbrokshire,' we have largely availed ourselves throughout these present pages.   George Owen appears to have come of a stout old country stock.   His father is said to have died a centenarian, after begetting a family of some twenty children.   Both George Owen and his father before him held the ancient and honourable office of Lord of Kemaes.

Taking leave of this historical spot, we now drop into a hollow bowery lane that hugs the course of the Dûad Stream, and passes through the rough intricate country known as Pencelly Forest, where in olden times the lord of the manor claimed right of pannage for hogs, with the wild honey and sparhawks found in the forest.   Our route now leads near Court, where Martin de Turribus, the conqueror of Kemaes, had a lordly dwelling, which, according to George Owen, 'seemeth to have been a house both of account and strengthe.'

A short half-hour later we find ourselves pacing the single 'street' of Eglwys-Erw, a picturesque village said to derive its name from the church having been built upon a plot of land measuring an acre. Fenton, on the other hand, attributes the origin of the name to a certain St. Erw, whose chapel, containing the tomb of the patron saint, used to stand in a corner of the churchyard. In olden times the peasant folk were averse to being buried in this chapel, owing to the prevalent superstition that their bodies were liable to be mysteriously ejected at dead of night, because, forsooth, St. Erw would brook no bedfellow!

Passing on between the neat, whitewashed cottages, we come to Sergeants' Inn, whose bow-windowed front stands near the upper end of the village. The somewhat unusual title of this hostelry is derived from the fact that, in earlier days, it was customary for the gentlemen of the Bar when 'on circuit' to foregather here; and the building next the inn is still called the Sessions House. At Sergeants' Inn is to be seen a small chest-lid, incised with the rather enigmatical legend: I.H.S, PRESTAT ESSE PROMETHEVS QUAM EPIMETHEUM, 1603.

Eglwys-Erw Church is soon disposed of; for it has been completely modernized, and bereft of any noteworthy features it may formerly have contained.

We now approach the confines of the parish of Eglwys-wen, or Whitechurch; a parish where adders are commonly reputed to be, like snakes in Iceland, absolutely unknown.

There is a curious tradition anent the yokels of Whitechurch parish. Says our trusty friend George Owen, 'In ancient times in this parish the Meanest and simplest Sort of people, yea the plain plough-men, were Skillful at chess play; they never being dwelling out of their Parish, but unlitterate, and brought up at the plough and Harrow altogether.' One would be curious to learn how it came to pass that these simple folk, dwelling in this remote Welsh parish, acquired such an unlooked-for reputation.

23

But the day is waxing old, and it is still a far cry to our night's bivouac at Newport. So, putting the best foot foremost, we speed along the highroad for a couple of miles or so, until, near a huge old earthwork ycleped Castell Mawr, we diverge to the left, cross a pretty streamlet, and get a direction from a passer-by to the famous cromlech at Pentre-Evan.

Standing in an open field, on the northern slope of the strange-looking hill called Carnedd Meibion Owen, this wonderful structure is undoubtedly the finest cromlech to be found in the Principality.

The gigantic capstone that forms the roof measures some 16 feet in length, by half as much across ; its longer axis lying, roughly speaking, north and south.   Beneath it stand four upright stones, tall enough to permit of a horseman passing beneath the cromlech. A closer inspection shows that two only of these standing stones support the weight of the capstone ; and their upper ends, being shaped like a narrow wedge, appear pointed when seen from the position whence our sketch was taken.

This noble relic of the prehistoric past has, under the Ancient

Monuments Protection Act, been enclosed within a tall iron fence, which, if not exactly a pleasing feature in itself, will doubtless preserve the cromlech from further abuse and injury.

Soft white mists are stealing athwart the vale of Nevern, and cling-ing around the skirts of the lower foot-hills, as we wend our way back to quarters at Newport town. Glancing in the direction whence we have come, the cloud-wreaths gathered around the shoulders of Precelly glow crimson under the rays of the declining sun, as he sinks into the pallid sea away beyond Dinas Head ; and by the time we arrive at our *rendezvous,* Darkness has spread her wings o'er the dusky landscape.

   *   *   *   *   *   *

The next morning sees us early under way, and well on the road to Kilgerran, ere the sun has climbed high enough to make matters un-pleasantly warm for the wayfarer. Beyond Nevern we pass near the lonely deserted chapel of Bayvil, and, after a long spell of steady collar-work, get some fine vistas of varied landscape near the old grass-grown barrows called Crugau Kemaes.

At the crossways farther on we are a matter of 500 feet above the sea, with Monington village on our left, and the church and ruined castle of Llantood away to the right. Then, as we near Kilgerran, we notice an old boundary-stone under the hedgerow, bearing a few half-obliterated lines anathematizing him who should venture to remove this landmark, the original purpose of which has probably long since been forgotten.

Passing under a railway arch, we soon descry Kilgerran Church, standing on the brink of a narrow ravine that opens towards the Teivy. St. Llawddog, from whom this church inherits its euphonious patronymic, appears to have been a saint of some local celebrity, for his name crops up at more than one place in the immediate neighbourhood.

With the exception of its gray old tower, Kilgerran Church has been entirely rebuilt, and calls for no particular notice. In the grave-yard stands a venerable monolith, much older than the church itself. The weathered surface of the stone is scored with those Ogham characters, so fascinating to the antiquarian mind ; these hieroglyphics have been deciphered as follows: TRENGUSSI FILI HIC IACIT. Unfortunately, a large portion of the *maenhir* is sunk below the level of the ground, thus rendering a thorough examination of its surface impracticable.

To eyes fresh from the beauties of Nevern, the long, rambling street of Kilgerran offers anything but an inviting appearance, being flanked by meagre unkempt dwellings, with but one or two cottages of more antique mould in the older portion of the village.

Despite the humble, not to say squalid, aspect of the place, there was a time when Kilgerran held a position of no small consequence. A borough town, governed by portreeve, aldermen and burgesses, its 'court-leet' and 'view of frankpledge' held their annual meetings at Kilgerran ; while many another time-honoured privilege bore witness to a state of things that has long since passed away.

In those piping times, it was customary for each newly-elected burgess to prove his fitness for office by draining *at one draught* a horn of strong Welsh ale ; the Corporation horn used on such occasions holding fully a pint and a half of liquor !

We now make our way to the castle ruins, which occupy the brow of a lofty cliff overhanging the deep gorge of the Teivy. The existing remains of Kilgerran Castle consist of two massive round towers, separating the outer from the inner bailey, with considerable fragments of the gatehouse.

The entire fabric is plain, and very massively constructed, showing little or no trace of ornamentation ; the few doorways and windows that remain being arched in a primitive fashion, without the use of the customary keystone. A rough stone wall encircles the precipitous scarp next the river, a portion of which fell down suddenly many years ago, having been undermined by the excavations of the quarrymen.

Kilgerran Castle appears to have been founded at a very remote period, though the existing structure is probably not older than the beginning of the thirteenth century. In Powell's ' History of Cambria,'

we read how, Henry I. having granted to Strongbow the lands of
Cadwgan ap Blethyn, the great Earl ' builded a faire castel at a place
callyd Dyngeraint, where Roger Montgomerie had begonne a castel
before tyme.' Its subsequent history is unimportant, and Kilgerran
Castle has at last succumbed to the shocks of time and the more
devastating hand of man, who appears to have regarded its ancient
walls in the light of a convenient quarry.

Looking out across the deep vale of Teivy, we can see the mansion
of Coedmore amidst its ensheltering woodlands. It is said that, in olden
times, a fishing-net was stretched athwart the river just below the
mansion, a line being attached to the net and connected to a bell,
which rang in the house to give notice to the inmates when a catch of
salmon had been effected.

The clear, unsullied waters of the Teivy, have ever been a favourite
haunt of the king of
fishes. Giraldus Cam-
brensis asserts that
' The noble river Teivy
abounds, more than any
river of Wales, with the
finest Salmons; and it
has a productive fishery
near Kilgerran.'

That curious craft
the ancient British
coracle is a familiar

A TEIVYSIDE CORACLE.

object to all dwellers on Teivyside, where from days immemorial it has
been employed by the fisher folk in the pursuit of their time-honoured
calling.

The coracle, or *corwg* as it is called in Wales, is somewhat of an
oval shape, but is raised high and flattened at the bows. The frame-
work consists of split rods forming a sort of basket-work, over which
tarred canvas is stretched, though in olden times cowhide was used for
this purpose; hence the ancient coracle weighed considerably more

than the modern one, and this explains the old Welsh adage, *Llwyth gwr ei Gorwg* (A man's load is his coracle). The seat is a stout ash-plank, and through it a loop or sling is twisted by which the owner carries his coracle upon his back, the wooden rails with which the seat is provided acting as a basket to carry the fish. The method of carrying the little craft is shown in the sketch at head of the present chapter.

Notwithstanding its great breadth of beam, it is by no means easy for a novice to propel the coracle by means of its single paddle; indeed, his efforts are likely to be brought to an untimely end by a plunge in the cold, clear depths of the Teivy.

After this digression, we will now take a stroll by Teivyside; descending from the village by a steep pathway beside some humble cottages and heaps of quarry refuse. As a result of certain ancient privileges, the townsfolk have gradually converted this portion of the left bank of the Teivy into a succession of slate quarries, whose ragged talus of *débris* encumbers the water's edge; a sorry substitute for the luxuriant groves that greet the eye wherever Nature has been allowed fair play.

KILGERRAN FERRY

Pursuing this rough track for about a furlong, we turn to the rightabout, and obtain a fine view of the castle lording it above a pretty reach of the river; and thence pursue a path that hugs the brink of the stream. After passing the last and deepest of the slate-mines, which has been carried far below the river-bed, we enjoy a still more charming glimpse of the grand old ruins enfolded amongst richly wooded hills, all mirrored in an unruffled sheet of water at a point where the ferry-boat lies moored beside the grassy bank.

Thenceforward our footpath meanders amidst the magnificent groves of oak, beech and ash, that adorn the estate of Castle Malgwyn;

KILGERRAN CASTLE FROM THE TEIFY.

their graceful forms reflected in the still, dark reaches of the placid Teivy, which hereabouts affords some of the finest river scenery to be found in all wild Wales.

Onwards to Llechrhyd Bridge, whose ivy-mantled arches, backed by the lodge and woodlands of the park, form a 'likely' subject for the artist's pencil.

The village, with its snug waterside inn beloved of anglers, has a very seductive air about it ; but we must not linger here, for these transpontine lands lie without the bounds of Pembrokeshire, and are therefore *taboo* to us.   So, striking away in the direction of the south, we traverse the spacious demesne of Castle Malgwyn, getting a

· LLECHRHYD ·
· BRIDGE ·

peep of the mansion set amidst dark, umbrageous woodlands ; our approach causing the startled bunnies to skirmish away helter-skelter into the bracken coverts as we pass.

The return route to Kilgerran lies through a pleasant vale, with

· CASTLE
MALGWYN ·

young oak-coppices upon the one hand, and a marshy reed-grown watercourse upon the other.

     *   *   *   *   *   *

Setting forth by a different route upon the morrow's morn, a row downstream from Kilgerran introduces us to some charmingly diversified reaches of the swift-flowing Teivy. After passing below the wooded slopes of Coedmore, our little craft threads the rocky channel as it twists, now this way, now that, through the broken undulating country, affording ever some fresh variation of the lovely changing landscape, to which the castle ruins form an imposing centre.

Presently we emerge upon broad tidal flats, where groups of cattle are browsing amidst the lush sedgy herbage. Shooting under Cardigan Bridge, we open out that final reach of the river where, in the words of George Owen, ' Teivy saluteth St. Dogmells, as it passeth to the sea.'

About a mile distant from the county-town of Cardigan, but on the Pembrokeshire side of the river, stands the before-mentioned village of St. Dogmaels. The little place is perched upon a rather steep declivity, its comely dwellings clambering up the slope, so that, from the top of the village, one's eye follows the course of the Teivy to the foam-fringed shores of Cardigan Bay, and the headland called Pen-Kemaes.

Here the cottage gardens are gay with heliotrope, fuchsias and hydrangea, which brave the winter out in the more sheltered corners; while the full-rigged flagstaffs that rise amidst the garden plots bespeak the nautical proclivities of the residents.

This village derives its name from the ancient Welsh monastery of St. Dogmaels, which stood about a mile away at a place still bearing the name of Yr Hên Mynachlog (the Old Monastery). Of this venerable structure, founded by Robert de Turribus, but scanty traces now remain, in the shape of a few ivy-mantled walls pierced with Gothic arches, whose crumbling stones retain the ballflower ornamentation of the Decorated period. The neighbouring parish church has, alas! been swept and garnished by iconoclastic hands, which have ruthlessly bereft the fabric of every feature of interest.

Our investigations completed, we betake ourselves to the Cardigan terminus, and travel thence over the branch line of the Great Western Railway as far as Crymmych-Arms Station. Beyond Kilgerran the line traverses some pretty furze-clad dingles, and, as we approach our destination, mounts in short, sharp curves towards the high ground that forms the watershed of northern Pembrokeshire.

24

From the summit level, some 700 feet above the sea, we command a noble prospect of the Precelly range, and the more remote hills about Newport Bay and Fishguard ; the effect being heightened by the sunset glow, while a brilliant rainbow spans the purple clouds that brood over the loftier crests of the distant mountains.

At Crymmych we avail ourselves of such accommodation as the wayside inn affords, intending to start away bright and early upon the morrow's explorations.

CROMLECH AT NEWPORT.

CHAPTER XI.

THE BROAD grassy slopes of Fryn-y-Fawr, (or Vrenny Vawr, as they pronounce it), a big isolated hill to the east of Crymmych-Arms, afford a pleasant morning's stroll, with a widespreading outlook at the end of it. The mountain road by which we approach the monticle follows the course of the ancient trackway called Fordd-Fleming, which we presently exchange for the open, heathery hillside; going as we please for the tall green tumulus that marks the summit.

Save towards the west, where the higher Precelly range intercepts the view, the prospect is wide and unrestricted, comprising nearly the whole of Pembrokeshire, with its setting of silvery sea, and a vast stretch of South Wales, including the peninsula of Gower; while the northern horizon is bounded by the remote Northwallian hills, amongst which, if the day be clear, the peak of Snowdon may possibly be distinguished.

Descending by the opposite end of the hill, we pass a small homestead, whose name indicates that the source of the Nevern River is near at hand.

Somewhere within the flanks of Fryn-y-Fawr, there lies hid (according to the tradition of the countryside) a leaden casket packed full with untold gold. The *genius loci* that guards this mysterious treasure takes the form of a violent tempest, which bursts, in thunder and lightning, around the head of the man who is foolhardy enough to seek to possess himself of the forbidden prize.

Returning to Crymmych-Arms, we settle up accounts with mine hostess—a simple process in these parts, often arranged without the formality of a 'bill,'—and set forth anew upon our wanderings.   The old trackway again forms our route, leading us past the site of a rude monument called Croes Mihangel, and thence across the heather-clad shoulders of Foel Trigarn, the easternmost spur of Precelly, which, as its name implies, is crowned with three cairns, surrounded by the stony ramparts of an ancient British stronghold.

THE SKIRTS OF PRECELLY.

The mountain vale opening out upon our left holds the springs of the eastern Cleddau, a stream that, after forming for some miles the county-boundary, passes below picturesque Llawhaden, and flows onwards amidst the rich woodlands of Slebech and Picton Castle, to merge in the broad, tidal waters of Milford Haven.

For the next few miles we enjoy a breezy tramp athwart the wild, uncultivated shoulders of Precelly—'Parcilly the Proud,' to use old Drayton's phrase.   In his own quaint fashion, George Owen thus describes these famous hills : ' The chiefest and principall mountaine of this shire is Percellye, which is a long ridge or rancke of mountaines runninge East and West ; beginninge above Penkellyvore, where the first mounte of highe land thereof is called Moel Eryr, and so passinge Eastward to Comkerwyn (being the highest parte of yt), runneth East to Moel Trygarn and to Llanvirnach.'

So far George Owen. Meanwhile we trudge onward across the springy turf, avoiding here a stretch of dusky bogland feathered with white tufts of cotton-grass, yonder a huge pile of weather-stained boulders, riven and tossed asunder by the tempests of ten thousand winters. One of these rugged cairns is known as King Arthur's Grave ; another bears a Welsh name signifying the ' rocks of the horsemen ' ; indeed, every feature of the landscape has its story or legend for the imaginative Cymro.

Rounding the head of a lonely glen, a rough but sufficiently easy ascent lands us beside the cairn that marks the summit of Foel Cwm Cerwyn, the loftiest peak of Precelly, and the highest ground in all broad Pembrokeshire. ' This mountaine,' says George Owen, ' is so highe and farre mountid into the ayre that, when the countrey about is faire and cleere, the toppe thereof wilbe hidden in a cloude, which of the inhabitantes is taken a sure signe of raigne to follow shortelie, whereof grewe this proverbe :

'" When Percellye weareth a hatte,
    All Penbrokeshire shall weete of that." '

Standing well apart, and removed from the mass of loftier South Welsh hills, the view from Precelly top is both extensive and interesting. Near hand, one's gaze wanders across a vast expanse of rather monotonous, treeless landscape, until the attention is arrested by the lake-like reaches of Milford Haven, spreading like crooked fingers far into the heart of the land.

South and west the sea encompasses all, with Gower lying far away upon the Bristol Channel, and perhaps a faint outline of the cliffs of Devon verging the remote horizon. The isolated hills overlooking St.

Davids are easily identified, flanked by a broad stretch of St. Bride's Bay, and its group of guardian islets. Strumble Head thrusts its tempest-torn crags seawards into Cardigan Bay, whose coast-line trends away league upon league with infinite gradation to where, softened by the humid, brine-laden atmosphere,

'The gray, cloud-cradled mountains spread afar.'

Newport Bay, lying under the lee of Dinas Head, looks as though one might cast a stone into its calm waters; and upon turning our gaze inland, the eye loses itself amidst the many-folding hills, as they rise in soft undulations to the dusky highlands of Glamorganshire.

We now push on along the crest of the moorland, striking once more into the course of the so-called Flemings' Way. After the manner of most early roads, this ancient trackway runs athwart the open highlands, avoiding the hollow places; and although much of it has been obliterated by the ploughshare, and the gradual advance of cultivation, its course may still be traced in the less-frequented localities, as it wends its way up country from the site of old Menapia towards the county-town of Carmarthen.

An ancient warrant of Sir Nicholas Martin, referring to the use of this old mountain road by the Flemish colony, observes: 'And well they might make this unusual waie for their passage, for that, passinge alonge the toppe of the highest hill, they might the better descrie the pryvie ambushes of the Countrye people, which might in streightes and woodds annoy them.'

At a place appropriately called the Pass of the Winds, we fall in with the main road as it crosses the hills from Haverfordwest to Cardigan. This we descend for a matter of half a mile, passing across a heathery upland ycleped the Hill of the Unstrung-Bows, until we come to Tafarn Bwlch, a humble wayside alehouse some thousand feet or so above sea-level.

Looking out across a broad brown reach of moorland, the eye detects a sort of rude stone causeway, curving amidst rush-grass and scattered peat-hags. This is known as Bedd-yr-Avangc, or the

Beaver's Grave ; *à propos* of which it is worthy of note that Giraldus Cambrensis mentions the beaver as abounding in his day on Teivyside, while more than one venerable legend locates this amphibious quadruped in the *llyns* and streams throughout wild Wales.

Arrived at Tafarn Bwlch, we call for such cheer as the lowly inn can supply; but the bill of fare proves somewhat scanty, for, in the words of the great lexicographer, 'of provisions its negative catalogue is very copious.' The goodwife, however, rises to the occasion, and regales us with a repast such as appetites sharpened by lusty mountain air make short enough work of. Then we burn incense to the drowsy god in a nook of the chimney-place, where a peat-fire glows untended upon the ample hearth.

Starting forth again like giants refreshed, we breast the stony ascent that leads to the pass amidst a sharp squall of wind and rain, which drags in a darkening veil athwart the lonesome landscape, blotting now this, now that familiar landmark from the view.

From the head of the pass we descend into the vale of the infant Syvynvy, rounding the broad green slopes of the Eagles' Hill, the westernmost buttress of the Precelly range. At the crossways we bear to the left, with the disused windmill of the slate quarries showing conspicuously upon a neighbouring hill.

Pushing on towards Maenclochog, we pass near the defunct Rosebush Station, on the line of the Maenclochog railway, which at present is undergoing in leisurely fashion a process of reconstruction. Indeed, in the matter of slowness, the builders of this line may fairly claim to have 'broken the record,' for 'tis whispered that seventeen years' work has added little more than four miles to the length of the railway!

Be that as it may, we now make our entry into the village of Maenclochog, a bleak-looking place enough, where the storm-rent trees beside the roadway attest the violence of the winter gales that sweep across these bare, lofty uplands.

Towards the farther end of the village, at a widening of the ways, stands the parish church, a structure of no great antiquity, dedicated to St. Mary. The clergyman, who has ministered here for upwards of thirty years, now courteously introduces us to the well-tended interior, the most noteworthy feature of which is a plain old font, with a singular cup-shaped recess upon its eastern face, the purpose of which we are quite at a loss to conjecture.

St. Mary's Church has no tower, but at the western end rises a low turret containing a musical peal of bells. It is a remarkable fact, indeed, that throughout this mountain district church towers are conspicuous by their absence; whereas, in the English country farther south, the tall slender bell-tower usually forms one of the most noticeable features of the parish church.

A marble cross used, we are informed, to adorn the chancel gable; but this has long since been removed to the limbo of things forgotten.

In olden times, it was customary at Maenclochog to draw the water for baptism from St. Mary's Well, a natural spring that rises just without the village. Near to this well are some tumbled stones, that once supported a large horizontal slab. Tradition tells that this stone, when struck, gave forth a loud ringing sound, which did not cease until the water from the holy well had been brought into the church. Hence the name of Maenclochog, which, being interpreted, signifies the village of the 'ringing rock.' It is much to be regretted that this curious object was destroyed many years ago, because, forsooth, the sound thereof was supposed to frighten passing horses!

At the foot of the village stands a large, rambling inn, backed by the singularly artificial-looking rocks known as 'the Castle,' whence the house takes its title. In a country where lodgings of any sort are so few and far between, the wayfarer may do worse than pitch his camp for a night in these unassuming quarters.

The way to Llandilo leads us through a hollow dingle, where a brawling trout-stream rushes along beneath cool, shadowy beech woods; while every here and there a glimpse of the purple hills adds variety to the scene.

Passing by Temple-Druid, the site of a now destroyed cromlech, we arrive at Llandilo, where we search in vain for the church; for this sparsely-peopled parish has been merged into that of Maenclochog, in consequence of which the sacred edifice has been allowed to fall into disrepair, and is now represented by a few crumbling walls smothered in rank, untended ivy.

Crossing the stone stile that gives access to the churchyard, we espy upon its southern side a slab of greenstone bearing, in rudely-chased letters, the inscription : COIMAGNI FILI CAVETI. A similar stone near the east end of the ruined chancel has also its superscription, which reads : ANDAGELLI IACIT; with a fainter line, possibly FILI CNOI, below ; and over all a cross with tridented terminations.

But the pride of the place is ' St. Teilo's skull,' which is treasured at the adjacent farmhouse. This curious relic was formerly held in high esteem as a cure for all manner of sickness, water being drawn from the saint's well, and drunk out of the skull. The virtue of the draught was supposed to consist in its being administered by the eldest son of the house of Melchior, then, as now, the hereditary custodian of St. Teilo's skull. Onwards to Llangolman, the country is crumpled up into a succession of hills and narrow, rocky dingles, whereby the numerous streamlets that enliven this locality find an outlet from the foothills of Precelly. In one of these dingles is St. Teilo's Well, a wayside spring frequented by that saint in days of yore.

Llangolman Church, perched on its isolated monticle, presents a sorry spectacle of desecration and decay ; its windows battered and broken, its roof open to the vault of heaven, while the rusty bell hangs cracked and useless in the dilapidated turret.

As we approach Monachlogddu, the landscape assumes a thoroughly Welsh appearance. A clear trout-stream, that comes rippling and dancing down the glen from the dark brown ridge of the moorlands, is here put to turn the wheel·of a little flannel-mill. In response to our request, the goodman describes in broken English the simple processes of manufacture, and explains the movements of his archaic machinery. Then, after a glance at the lowly parish church, dedicated to St. Dogmael, we bid adieu to the village of the Black Monastery, and take to the road again.

The neighbouring village of Llanvirnach is said to derive its name

25

from the following circumstance. When the good St. Byrnach was making his pilgrimage through this portion of the country, he could at first obtain no better quarters than a cowshed ; thus, as the story goes, arose the name of Llanbeudy, the Church of the Cowhouse. The next day the saint fared even worse, for, coming to Cilmaenllwyd, he was obliged, for lack of better accommodation, to repose beneath the gray cromlech that gives the place its name. The third night, however, St. Byrnach came to a place where he was accorded a kindly welcome, and provided with a comfortable night's lodging. Overcome with gratitude for this hospitable reception, St. Byrnach declared the place should ever after bear his own name ; and hence it is called to this day Llanvirnach, or the Church of St. Byrnach.

But to return to Maenclochog. Retracing our steps through the village, we bear away to the left, and presently come to a roadside spring called St. Byrnach's Well, a resort of that ubiquitous saint.

Our route now leads past Poll-tax Inn, and follows the course of the Via Julia, that ancient highway by which the Roman legions traversed this wild, uncivilized territory, from Maridunum, the present town of Carmarthen, to their remotest settlement at Menapia, on the shores of Whitesand Bay.

Diverging from the mountain road that marks the route of the Roman highway, we turn aside into a cross-country lane, pass several cairns and cromlechs, and presently come to Little Newcastle, a mean, unkempt village, presenting few attractions for the wayfarer.

At Little Newcastle was born a certain Bartholomew Roberts, who, about a century ago, made some noise in the world as a successful filibuster. In company with his fellow-countryman Howel Davies, (as big a rascal as himself), this notorious freebooter sailed the high seas arrayed in priceless silks and jewels galore—as pretty a pair of desperadoes as ever hoisted the skull-and-crossbones flag, or graced the yardarm of a man-o'-war.

From Little Newcastle we make the best of our way to St. Dogwells, a mite of a place tucked into an elbow of the stream, and overlooked upon the north by a rock-strewn eminence called Castell

Conyn. Through the woods of Sealyham we pass on to Letterston; noting a curious piscina in the church, and an effigy which long passed muster as that of St. Leotard, its founder.

Beyond the old chapel at Ford, where the Roman highway crossed the river, the road winds through the heart of the gorge amidst a wealth of bracken and purple heather; the huge form of Trefgarn Rock towering high aloft on our right. With the brawling Cleddau, half hidden by copsewoods, tumbling along through the hollow of the glen, the whole forms as romantic a bit of scenery as any to be found in the county.

At the adjacent village of Trefgarn, that great Welsh patriot and freelance, the famous Owen Glyndwr, is said to have first seen the light; an event that took place about the middle of the fourteenth century. Certain strange phenomena that were observed at the time of his birth, were turned to full account by this enterprising adventurer; hence Shakespeare, in his play of ' Henry IV.,' puts into the mouth of Glyndwr the proud words:

> ' At my birth
> The front of heav'n was full of fiery shapes;
> The goats ran from the mountains, and the herds
> Were strangely clamorous in the frighted fields:
> These signs have marked me extraordinary,
> And all the courses of my life do show
> I am not in the roll of common men.'

Alighting at Rudbaxton village, we step aside in order to visit the parish church. Upon the south side of the chancel, a pair of flat limestone arches open into what is known as the Howard Chapel, the eastern wall of which supports a large, seventeenth-century monument, commemorating various members of that honourable family.

The male and female figures beneath the arched recesses are represented as nearly the full size of life, habited in the costume of the period, and painted in a somewhat crude and barbaric manner. As may be seen in our sketch, every figure save one bears a human skull in its hand, thus recording in a suggestive way the decease of that individual.   One effigy alone is *minus* this grim feature, as it represents the lady in whose lifetime the monument was erected.

The panel beneath the central group bears the inscription, ' To the memory of James Howard of this Parish, Esq. who lyeth before this monument, and departed this life the 29th day of November Ano 1668, Aged 35 years.   Also the memory of Joanna, the Wife of James Howard, who erected this monument for her Deare friends and children,

THE HOWARD MONUMENT
AT RUDBAXTON

with the intent to Joyne partner to this Monument, and left this life. . . .'

The figure to the left represents George Howard, who died in 1665 ; those upon the right being Thomas and Mary, son and daughter of the central figures, who died, respectively, in 1682 and 1685.   A sundial upon the outer south wall of the Howard Chapel bears the initials J. H. and the date 1665.

Descending a hollow lane, we cross a stream and pass near the scanty ruins of Flether Hill, the ancient abode of the Haywards, whose tombstones we have seen in the church. Then, leaving the pleasant grounds of Withybush away upon our left, we presently strike the main road again at a place called Crowsnest, and thus approach the town of Haverfordwest by its long, transpontine suburb of Prendergast.

AT HAVERFORDWEST.

CHAPTER XII.

IT IS market day in Haverfordwest. The big travel-stained waggons of the wholesale traders, drawn by sturdy large-limbed horses, trundle slowly through the crowded streets of the old town; while the distinctive tones of the 'broad Harfat talk' greet the ear upon every side.

Wending our way down the steep High Street, we bear away to the right at the bottom of the hill, and traverse one of the oldest quarters of the town. Presently we descry a low-browed entrance opening upon the foot-path, the massive nail-studded door, with its quaint lion-head knocker, being enframed by liberally-moulded jambs. Passing beneath this ancient portal, we are admitted to an interior beautified by the rare old oaken stairway shown in our sketch; this stairway gives access to nicely panelled chambers, whose fireplaces retain their original blue Dutch tiles, painted with scenes from Biblical history.

To the rear of the dwelling-house stands a flour-mill of antiquated type; yet driving, withal, a brisk trade in its green old age. A well-trained old horse, the mainstay of the establishment, jogs round in the mill and supplies the motive power.

Stepping out to the rear, we find ourselves upon the riverside quay, along which we now take our way. Groups of bulky stone warehouses flank the grass-grown wharf, which presently opening out, reveals the Bristol Trader, a little semi-nautical inn, with its trim bit of garden-ground abloom with hollyhocks and nasturtiums; an old-time spot

OLD STAIRCASE AT HAVERFORDWEST

frequented by waterside gossips, and fraught with vague echoes from that wide outer world where men ' go down to the sea in ships.'

Hence we push on past the ruined priory to the diminutive village of Haroldstone, where some traces still exist of the ancient mansion that, for three successive centuries, was the ancestral home of the Perrots, one of the most notable old families of Pembrokeshire.

Vis-à-vis across the river Cleddau rises the parish church of Uzmaston ; a picturesque assemblage of roofs and gables, clustering around a quaint old saddle-backed tower. Uzmaston Church has,

within the last few years, been rescued from decay, and conscientiously restored by Mr. Lingen Barker, architect, of Hereford.

Skirting a bend of the river, we trudge through the woods to Freystrop, and enter upon a district pitted here and there with old mine-shafts. Over the water lies Boulston, where hard by the brink of the stream (perhaps a bowshot east from the desecrated church) rises a jumble of ivy-clad ruins, backed by a tangled thicket of old forest trees. Here lived the Wogans, a well-known family in days of yore, who adopted a wyvern as their crest from the following tradition.

Amidst the broad woodlands that formerly extended around the ancestral mansion, wild beasts of various kinds were supposed to roam at large. In the remotest depths of the forest lurked the dreaded basilisk, a formidable monster whose glance caused instant death to the ill-starred wight upon whom its gaze might rest, but which perished itself if first perceived by a man.

At last a certain bold fellow determined to rid the countryside of this objectionable beast. Causing himself to be shut up in a cask and rolled into the forest, he peeped through the bung-hole, and presently spied the basilisk without himself being seen. Thereupon the dreaded monster, giving vent to an unearthly yell that could be heard for miles around, fell down and perished upon the spot, so that the country-folk were no longer troubled by the molestations of the basilisk. A dragon legend, very similar to the above, is connected with the village of Mordiford in Herefordshire.

By-and-by, as we descend from the uplands, a broad reach of the tideway opens out right before us, where the twin streams of Cleddau merge into the widening Haven. Thus we enter the village of Langwm at its upper end, escorted by a rabble of noisy, unkempt urchins who cumber the narrow roadway.

Here, in the very heart of southern Pembrokeshire, stranded like a human jetsam upon one of the inmost recesses of Milford Haven, we find an isolated community, whose speech and physiognomy alike proclaim their Teutonic origin. Imagination conjures up those far-away times, when the sturdy immigrants from over seas—ancestors of these hardy fisher-folk—pushed their advance up the winding waterway, despite the desperate onslaughts of the Britons, who, fighting for hearth and home, ' rolled on like the billows of a retiring tide with noise, fury, and devastation, but on each retreat yielded ground to the invaders.'

In their own thoroughgoing fashion, the newcomers set to work to construct a chain of castles to guard their hard-won territory ; and thus, protected from the restless foe, grew up those peaceful villages and smiling homesteads, surrounded by orchards, fields, and pasture lands, that have earned for this portion of the county its title of the Little England beyond Wales.

But *revenons à nos moutons,* for it is time to look about us.

A curious place is Langwm, and a singular race are the people that dwell therein. Small 'butt-and-ben' cottages, some thatched, some slated, others roofed with hideous corrugated iron, compose the major portion of the village; which straggles down a narrow combe, whose lower reaches open upon an oozy elbow of the river.

The women, as a rule, are conspicuous by their absence; for they are for the most part abroad, hawking fish and oysters up and down the country. Clad in stout pea-jackets and warm blue homespun skirts, worn short for travelling the rough country roads, these hard-working women seem to belong to some alien race, as they elbow their way through the crowded streets of Tenby or Haverfordwest.

LANGWM FISHWIVES.

The Langwm people have, indeed, always kept very much to themselves, discouraging alliances with outsiders; nor until recent years would they even permit their girls to go out as domestic servants. In the old unregenerate days, courtship and marriage were attended with certain curious, primitive customs— customs which, to say the least, were 'more honoured in the breach than the observance.' One way and another, this singular people forms an interesting little community, which appears to have preserved intact to the present day much of the manners and customs of the early Flemish colonists.

Langwm Church is dedicated to St. Hierom. The little edifice stands, as its name implies, in a hollow combe near Milford Haven. To reach it we cross a bit of rough unenclosed greensward, littered over with oyster-shells, upon which, according to the local story, the village itself is built.

The interior of this church is enriched with some interesting Decorated features ; notably a canopied niche and piscina of unusual type, upon the eastern wall of the north chapel, or transept.

Under an ogee canopy, in the gable wall of the same chapel, lies the effigy of a De la Roche (or Dolly Rotch in the vernacular), to whose family this chapel formerly belonged.   The figure is that of a Crusader, clad in full armour and sword in hand ; the face is both handsome and expressive, and the head reposes upon a plumed helmet.   The thong of

. LAWRENNY
  CASTLE .

the boot, twisted around the leg, bears some resemblance to a serpent ; and hence this monument is pointed out as that of the founder of Roch Castle, who, as an old story avers, met his death through the bite of a 'loathlie worme.'

Near Langwm the twin Cleddaus merge into the broad bosom of the tideway ; becoming, as old George Owen says, ' both a salt sea of a myle broade and xvi myles longue before they forsake their native Countrie, . . . and then by Curse of nature yeald themselves to the sea, the endinge of all Rivers.'

We now cross the ferry, and, after passing through Marteltewi, bear

away in a southerly direction *en route* for Lawrenny. The latter is a
pleasant-looking village, with comely cottages concentrated around the
parish church of St. Caradoc, whose tall, ivy-mantled tower rises close
at hand, overshadowed by a grove of stately elms where the rooks are
making merry.

To the rear of the church the ground slopes up to a boss of open
land, fringed with a thick growth of copsewood, and almost cut off from
the circumjacent country by two converging 'pills,' or tidal creeks.

Pursuing a field-path that skirts the stream at the base of the
monticle, we stroll through the park-like demesne of Lawrenny Castle,

a handsome modern edifice, whose soaring turrets and battlements make a brave show amidst the silvan scenery.

Making our way to a handful of cottages beside a neglected quay, we now select a likely-looking craft, and pull across the Western Cleddau to the ruins of Benton Castle; whose ivy-clad battlements scarcely overtop the redundant oak woods, that come feathering down to the very brink of the stream.

Little remains of the fabric save the principal tower, the base of which is circular in form, the upper works being corbelled out and fashioned into an octagon. With the arched gateway, flanked by a portion of a second drum-tower, these crumbling ruins form a picturesque group, whose features are almost lost amidst the luxuriant foliage that runs riot over all.

Benton Castle appears never to have been more than a mere outpost, planted to guard the passage of the Western Cleddau, and forming a link in the chain of strongholds to guard this remote English settlement. History has little to tell about its past, but the castle is reputed to have been originally built by Bishop Beck. It was at one time surrounded by an extensive deer park, a portion of the ancient estate of Williamstown, which, as George Owen tells us, was sequestrated to the Crown upon the attainder of Sir John Perrot.

After groping about for some time, in vain endeavour to obtain a satisfactory view, we at last secure a sketch of Benton Castle; and then, recrossing the water, make the best of our way back again to Lawrenny.

Inns, good, bad or indifferent, appear to be an 'unknown quantity' in this highly-respectable village; but an enterprising grocer rises to the occasion, and plays the *rôle* of Boniface as one to the manner born.

Upon resuming our peregrinations, we set our course for Land-shipping Ferry; while the gathering clouds, brooding over the darkening landscape, warn us to make ready against the 'useful trouble of the rain.' With a sudden swirl the gale descends upon us, sweeping through the straining tree-tops, and lashing up the waters of the creek into the semblance of a miniature *Maelström.*

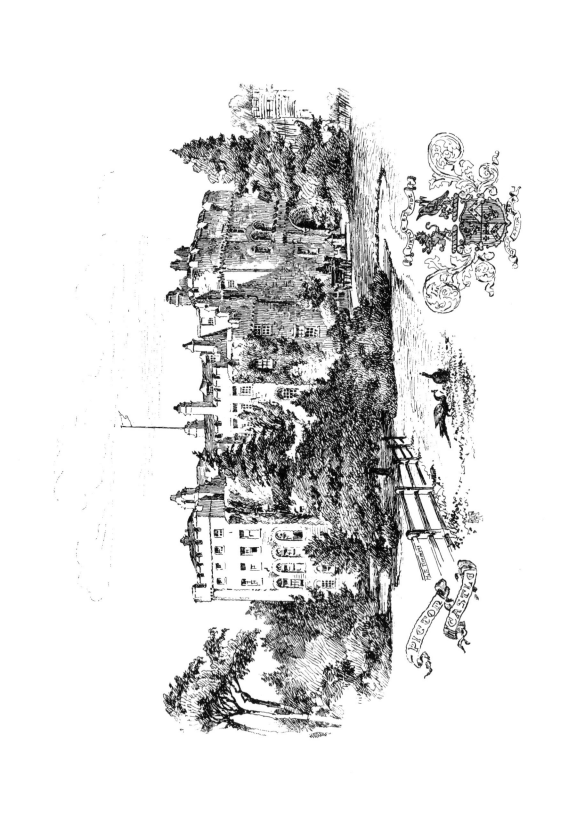

Scudding for shelter to a rustic alehouse, we soon make ourselves at home in the deep, oaken settle beside the chimney-corner; discussing the day's adventures over a mug of home-brewed ale, while the fumes of the 'noxious weed' float upwards to the ripening flitches, that hang from the smoke-begrimed rafters overhead.

Half an hour later finds us once more under way, with the sunshine blinking out again through the tail of the retreating storm, and the raindrops glistening like diamonds on every bush and hedgerow:

> 'Sweet is sunshine through the rain,
> All the moist leaves laugh amain;
> Birds sing in the wood and lane
> To see the storm go by, O!
>
> 'Overhead the lift grows blue,
> Hill and valley smile anew;
> Rainbows fill each drop of dew,
> And a rainbow spans the sky, O!'

Running us ashore near some cottages, at a picturesque nook of the Haven, the ferryman now puts us in the way for Picton; which is reached after a brisk twenty minutes' tramp through the leafy glades of a deep, sequestered dingle.

It would be difficult to image anything more attractive than the situation of Picton Castle. Crowning the brow of a gentle declivity, the stately pile is sheltered from the north and east by groves of forest trees, and mighty banks of rhododendrons; while upon its southern side a beautiful expanse of the home-park rolls away, 'in emerald slopes of sunny sward,' to a broad, land-locked reach of Milford Haven.

In conjunction with the neighbouring estate of Slebech, Picton Park comprises a vast extent of open, park-like land, the haunt of game and wild-fowl; while the river front affords miles of woodland strolls, with a charming variety of ever-changing prospects. What with boating and fishing galore, not to mention an occasional meet of fox and otter hounds, he must indeed be a fastidious sportsman who cannot find recreation in this favoured locality.

Picton Castle can boast a record unmatched in the annals of any other Southwallian fortalice ; for the place has never once been deserted, but has always been occupied by those who can claim direct descent from the original founder.

It was in the days of William Rufus (when Arnulph the Norman handed over the whole of the surrounding district to his trusty follower) that Sir William de Picton erected the first castle, and gave his own name to his newly-acquired possession. To his descendant, the good Sir John Philipps, the town of Haverfordwest is indebted for its fine old sandstone bridge, which he caused to be built at his own expense, and presented as a free gift to the borough. John Wesley and Sir Isaac Newton were numbered amongst his friends ; and a monument, erected to his memory by the grateful townsfolk, is to be seen in St. Mary's Church, Haverfordwest.

General Picton, of Peninsular War renown, was a famous scion of the same good stock. It is said that, owing to his influence abroad, large quantities of the best wine of Oporto found their way into many a Pembrokeshire cellar, where such a vintage had hitherto been a luxury unknown.

During the Civil Wars, Picton Castle was garrisoned and held for King Charles by Sir Richard Philipps, second baronet ; but was eventually surrendered (as the story goes) under the following circumstances.

One day during the course of the siege, a servant-maid was standing at an open casement in the eastern bastion with Sir Erasmus, the infant heir, upon her arm ; when a Parliamentary trooper rode up with a flag of truce, and presented a letter at the window. No sooner had the maid reached forward to take the missive, than, raising himself in the saddle, the soldier snatched the child from the nurse's arms, drew his sword, and threatened to slay the hope of Picton upon the spot, unless the castle were instantly surrendered.

Though much altered and extended in comparatively modern times, Picton Castle still presents an imposing and dignified appearance ; especially when viewed from the south-east side, whence our sketch is taken.

The entrance front (which is by far the oldest portion of the structure) retains the deeply-recessed portal, the rounded arches, quaint, archaic corbel-heads and narrow windows, that mark the enduring handiwork of the original Norman builders. Above the massive entrance porch rise the deep-set windows of the chapel; the handsome painted glass with which they are adorned, forming an appropriate memorial to a member of the family of Sir Charles and Lady Philipps, whose tragic death, in 1893, aroused the deep sympathy of the entire county.

Rounded bastions project at intervals from the main structure, which is of an oblong form, with a lofty wing flanking its western end. The moat, having no purpose to serve in these piping times of peace, has long since been filled up; and its place is now occupied by pleasant walks and *parterres*, varied by luxuriant shrubberies.

The interior of the castle contains numerous suites of apartments, disposed around a handsome and spacious hall, from whose lofty walls historic family portraits of various styles and periods look down upon the beholder.

At one end of the hall is a gallery communicating with the private chapel above mentioned; and several quaint, old-fashioned chambers, whose solid circular walls are of enormous thickness. The panelled floors and ceilings of these apartments are worthy of notice, as are their white marble chimney-pieces, delicately wrought in the Italian manner. From the recesses of the deep-set windows, we command a lovely prospect over the rich rolling woodlands of the park, encircled by a silvery reach of the Cleddau towards Landshipping Ferry.

Passing along the green alleys of the home-wood, we presently emerge upon a stretch of breezy downland, and forge ahead through whispering bracken and heather; while the sound of a woodcutter's axe and the distant bleating of sheep float lazily hitherward upon the calm, clear air.

Thence we plunge into a shadowy belt of greenwood that fringes the waterside; nor until we are nearing Slebech do these woodland glades roll back, and give place to the more open scenery of Baron de Rutzen's beautiful demesne.

27

The mansion and ruined church of Slebech occupy the site of a Commandery of the Knights of St. John of Jerusalem, who early in the twelfth century established a small community here, to collect funds for the purposes of that ancient fraternity. The creation of this Commandery appears to have been an event of considerable importance ; and we find such names as Maurice de Prendergast, the invader of Ireland, and Fitzgerald, the notorious Bishop of St. Davids, enrolled amongst its earliest benefactors.

Dedicated to St. John the Baptist, the old ruined church of the Knights-Templars stands in a low, sheltered situation, half surrounded by the waters of the Cleddau ; just one of those secluded spots that seem to have been congenial to the mediæval temperament. The main walls and arches of the fabric still remain fairly intact, and, like the western tower, are smothered in masses of rank, untended ivy.

A doorway in the northern face of the tower gives access, beneath a low-pitched, Gothic archway, to the interior of the church. This archway is surmounted by a decayed stone escutcheon, charged with certain armorial bearings which Fenton deciphered as 'arms quarterly, first and fourth a fesse dauncette, second and third a lion rampant.' A similar shield, at the apex of an upper window, displays the simple cross of the Order of St. John of Jerusalem.

The dismantled interior, carpeted with rank herbage and vaulted with the dome of heaven, looks picturesque in its decay. From the spot whence our sketch was taken, the old font is seen near at hand, overtopped by an arch giving access to a pretty side-chapel with traceried window, and a small piscina formed in the flank of the pillar. Through the open archway upon the right we gain a glimpse of the roofless, desecrated chancel. When Fenton was here, about the beginning of the present century, the latter was still covered with its wooden ceiling, fashioned into square compartments and ornamented at the crossings of the beams with floreated enrichments, conspicuous amidst which appeared the arms of the Barlow family.

At that time the Barlow monument occupied a prominent position against the south wall of the chancel, which may be easily identified

SLEBECH

OLD CHURCH

H.T.T. 189?

by the ragged stonework whence the structure has been torn away. This act of vandalism is much to be deplored, for the monument appears to have been an unusually handsome one, the effigies of Barlow and his lady reposing beneath a sumptuous canopy, surmounted by a blank escutcheon.

By some lucky chance these figures have escaped destruction, and are now safely stowed away in the vaults of Slebech new church. They are excellently carved in alabaster, that of the knight being of great size; his head with its long curling locks rests upon a helmet, while the collar and order of the Golden Fleece is suspended around his shoulders. Hence it is supposed that this figure represents a certain Roger Barlow, who in the reign of Henry VIII. travelled into Spain, and was employed by the Spanish monarch in his South American ventures.

The lady, whose effigy is apparently of somewhat earlier date than that of the male figure, is arrayed in a handsome robe, over which is drawn a gracefully flowing mantle; while her long, smooth hair, bound with a chaplet around the brows, falls upon either side about her sloping shoulders.

Foundations of ancient buildings are said to have been traced in the grounds, between the church and the neighbouring mansion; but nothing worthy of note has as yet seen the light of day.

Slebech House appears to have been erected at a period when architecture had fallen to about its lowest ebb; its yellow plastered walls being pierced with rows of featureless windows, and surmounted by meagre, meaningless battlements. Nevertheless, the spacious chambers command such charming vistas of woodland and shimmering waters, as to go far towards making amends for architectural shortcomings. The mansion has superseded a structure of no mean antiquity, but of its history, which was presumably quiet and uneventful, few records have survived to our times.

Some three miles to the northward of Slebech lies the obscure hamlet of Wiston; a place so small and insignificant, that it is by no means easy to picture it as the erstwhile head of the barony of Daugleddau, a borough town, and the home of the powerful Wogans.

Wiston, we are told, derives its name from a certain Wiz, or Wyzo, a Flemish immigrant of considerable influence, who built a castle here to protect the infant settlement; of this castle a portion of the keep or donjon-tower, and a ruined gateway, still remain in tolerable repair. After having been more than once beleaguered and destroyed, the place was dismantled and deserted at an early period; so that Wiston Castle plays but a minor part in the records of border warfare.

Of the Wogan family, who for many generations made Wiston their home, the most famous scion was Sir John of that ilk, who was Lord Chief Justice of England in the reign of Edward I. This Sir John, it may be noted *en passant*, took to himself the style and title of 'Lord of Pyketown.'

So much, then, for Wiston. We now set forth from Slebech, and jaunt along beside the Eastern Cleddau, with the broad umbrageous woods of Minwear combing down to the water's edge, upon the farther bank of the stream. Ere long the Vale of Cleddau begins to widen out, forming a comely, verdant strath, through which the highroad winds like a narrow ribbon as it takes its way towards Narberth. For the present, however, we give this road the go-by, and turn near Canaston bridge into a ruddy lane, which climbs by a gentle ascent to the crest of the ridgeway.

Down in the vale below, at a place bearing the name of St. Kennox, lived good Rees Pritchard, the famous Welsh divine, sometime Chancellor of St. Davids Cathedral, and author of a celebrated book entitled 'Canwyll y Cymro,' or the Welshman's Candle. Such was the fame of Pritchard's oratory, that the vast congregations who flocked to hear him preach overflowed the limits of the cathedral walls, and clustered thick as hiving bees in the great south porch, and around the precincts of the sacred building.

In about another mile, our lane suddenly debouches upon the broad, triangular grass-plot, that forms the village-green of time-honoured Llawhaden. Grouped around the green rise a number of old substantial homesteads—true 'homes of ancient peace'—whose low-browed lattice-windows look out upon a vasty duck-pond, over-shadowed by clumps of gnarled and weather-beaten firs.

LLAWHADEN CASTLE AND BRIDGE.

Turning to the right at the foot of the green, we fare along the village street until it terminates abruptly in a sort of *cul-de-sac*, where the majestic ruins of Llawhaden Castle seem to forbid our further progress.

The great Gatehouse, with its lofty drum towers flanking the boldly-arched portcullis, indicates the noble scale upon which the fortress was conceived. The eastern tower is still in a fair state of preservation, retaining the strong stone floors of its successive stages, though its fellow has been shorn of more than half its bulk. These towers are pierced with small but well-proportioned lancet-windows, apparently of Edwardian date, and the corbelled battlements are carried forward above the gateway, to form a *couloir* for pouring down molten lead upon the foe.

On passing beneath the lofty entrance archway, we are confronted by a well-proportioned Gothic doorway, with one small pointed window, little more than a loophole, in the wall beside it; these are the sole relics of the northern front, of which all else has fallen to decay. Near at hand rises a slender square tower, whose trefoil-headed windows and finely-worked mouldings point to a later period than that of the main structure. From its position and certain accessories, there is reason to suppose this tower contained the chapel of the castle, erected by Bishop Vaughan, who enlarged and beautified St. Davids Cathedral.

A group of flourishing ash-trees, which have sprung up wheresoever they listed, cast their chequered shade athwart the neglected courtyard; whilst pigs and poultry, from the adjacent farmstead, roam untended amidst the masses of fallen masonry, that cumber the ground in every direction.

Although perched on the brink of a steep declivity, the castle was protected by a moat which still remains intact, though sadly choked with tangled undergrowth and *débris*. This moat was supplied with water from a stream, which forms the large pond at the foot of the village.

28

Thomas Beck, Bishop of St. Davids, is said to have erected Llawhaden Castle, towards the close of the thirteenth century; but it is more than probable his building merely superseded a structure of earlier date.

This worthy prelate also founded, 'in his Villa de Llewhadyn, a little *Hospitium*, which he dedicated to the poor and needy;' devoting to its maintenance the revenues derived from his own lands. Thus Bishop Beck became the first Welsh patron of pilgrims, and supporter of the aged and infirm.

Of this very interesting foundation, all that has survived is a small building with vaulted roof, doorway, windows and a piscina, situated in a field on the outskirts of the village. This little edifice was in all probability the chapel of Beck's *hospitium*. A certain Friar William was entrusted with the charge of the establishment, both he and his brethren wearing a habit distinctive of their calling.

By the time of Owen Glyndwr, the castle appears already to have fallen into disrepair; as we read that the King gave orders for Llawhaden to be put into a state of defence, victualled, and furnished with a garrison.

Under the disastrous *régime* of Bishop Barlow, that rapacious prelate caused the lead to be stripped from off the castle roofs, even as he had done at the beautiful old palace of St. Davids. Thenceforth the stately fabric, exposed to the disintegrating forces of Nature, gradually succumbed to its misfortunes, and sank into the condition of an uninhabitable ruin.

At their castle of Llawhaden, the Bishops of St. Davids lived in true baronial style; the fortress constituting the *Caput Baroniæ*, by virtue of which they were entitled to representation in the Parliament of the realm.

Before taking leave of Llawhaden Castle, we secure the accompanying sketch of the great Gatehouse, whose hoary lichen-clad masonry, wreathed in clinging ivy, rises with bold and striking effect against the dark foliage of a neighbouring coppice.

Descending by a steep, hollow lane to the banks of Cleddau, we linger long about the old bridge and castle-mill to enjoy the placid beauty of the landscape, whose rich, subdued tints are enhanced by the radiance of a mellow autumn afternoon.

Looking upstream, the church forms the central feature of a pleasant, restful prospect; its picturesque tower reflected in the clear waters of the Cleddau, which rushes onward to tumble with refreshing roar over a weir close at hand. Amidst the hanging woodlands which clothe the castle-hill, we catch a glimpse of that ancient fortalice; while the lowing of kine comes pleasantly to the ear from the deep water-meadows down the vale.

We now bend our steps towards the parish church, noticing a simple wooden cross beside the wicket-gate, whereon is hung a lantern to guide the footsteps of the benighted flock, during the long, dark evenings of winter.

Llawhaden Church stands somewhat remote from the village, in a sequestered nook where the castle hill and the Cleddau leave scarce sufficient room for the little church to stand; insomuch that its chancel gable wellnigh overhangs the stream. Dedicated to St. Hugo, the sacred edifice contains the mutilated effigy of an ecclesiastic, commonly supposed to represent the patron saint, but more probably intended for Adam Houghton, Bishop of St. Davids, and co-founder with John o' Gaunt of St. Mary's College in that 'city.'

Houghton distinguished himself by enacting a statute to regulate the scale of wages, and the price of beer, on behalf of his faithful 'subjects;' while tradition avers that, having been excommunicated by the Pope for some misdemeanour or other, this intrepid prelate retaliated by excommunicating the Holy Father himself!

Inside the church we notice several curiously-sculptured corbels; besides a two-three quaint epitaphs reciting, in rather questionable English, the virtues and graces of certain local worthies.

The semi-detached tower presents a picturesque appearance, having, attached to its southern face, a square-shaped turret which, curiously enough, looks older than the tower itself. The internal construction of this tower is somewhat peculiar, and its belfry contains a triplet of sweet-toned bells.

It is, perhaps, worthy of note that Llawhaden is supposed to derive its name from St. Aeddan, a Pembrokeshire man by birth, and a disciple of St. David himself.

Having inspected an ancient cross, built into the eastern gable of the church, we now retrace our footsteps to the bridge, where, after searching for some time in vain owing to intervening foliage, we at last pitch upon a suitable spot for a sketch of that timeworn structure.

This done, we reluctantly turn our backs upon pretty Llawhaden, and fare away in the direction of Narberth, playing hide-and-seek with our shadows as they lengthen under the westering sun. Groups of lads and little lasses, homeward bound from school, linger in twos and threes by the rough laneside, where the bramble brakes are thickest; purple lips and stained pocket-handkerchiefs showing the blackberry season is now in full swing.

Anon we clamber over a tall step-stile, near a widespreading ash-tree whose singular form at once arrests the eye. After growing for some feet in a horizontal direction, the massive bole turns abruptly at a sharp right angle, and shooting skywards, straight as an arrow, branches out into a head of symmetrical foliage, like the trees in a Dutchman's garden.

Pushing on by a footpath that winds down towards a stream in the hollow of the vale, we presently stumble hot-foot upon a covey of part-ridges, who are up in a twinkling, and blustering away to the shelter of a neighbouring stubble-field; while the voice of an unseen threshing-machine, 'a-bummin' away like a buzzard clock,' palpitates through the drowsy air of the still, September afternoon.

Leaving St. Kennox away to our right, we now make for the village of Robeston Wathen; the choice lying between breasting the hill by a steep green field-path, or approaching in more leisurely fashion by way of the lane. The voting goes all in favour of the shorter route, which brings us out at a point near Robeston Church, whose tall, isolated tower is conspicuous for a long distance around. At the cross-roads near the village stands a group of wayside cottages, whose deep thatched roofs, and low porches embowered in honeysuckle and climbing plants, make a very charming picture.

Past the disestablished toll-gate, the road slants away down the bank to a bridge over a narrow streamlet. Thence ensues the long, steady ascent of Cock's Hill, which lands us eventually at a considerable altitude on the outskirts of Narberth; a place that, with the exception of its ruined castle, has little to commend it to wayfarers who, like ourselves, are 'in search of the picturesque.'

A town of some importance in bygone times, when its markets were resorted to by half the countryside, Narberth appears of late to have fallen upon degenerate days; the mail-coaches having deserted its grass-grown streets for ever, while the railway trains that have usurped their place give the unfortunate town the go-by, in favour of other and more enterprising communities.

Wending our way adown the long, featureless High Street, we pass on our left the broad front of the De Rutzen Arms, a large wayside posting-house, around whose weed-grown courtyard hang memories of the old coaching days. Then, leaving the parish church away to the right, and navigating some intricate lanes, we approach the outskirts of the town, and make the best of our way to the castle ruins.

Crowning the southward slope of the hill upon which the town is located, Narberth Castle occupies a position of considerable importance. The ruins of the fortress, though small, and devoid of striking features, are not without a certain picturesque appearance when seen from the Tenby road. It must, however, be confessed that 'distance lends enchantment to the view;' for the existing remains are of a very fragmentary nature, consisting of a few broken bastions, with some odds and ends of more or less dilapidated masonry.

At the time of the Norman Conquest, Narberth fell to the share of Sir Stephen Perrot, a follower of the redoubtable Arnulph de Montgomery. Although there is record of a castle here as long ago as the eleventh century, the present structure is certainly not of earlier date than the days of Sir Andrew Perrot, or, say, about the middle of the thirteenth century; indeed, the character of the existing work seems to point to its erection at an even later period.

In the reign of Edward III., Narberth Castle came into the possession of Roger Mortimer, the great Earl Marcher, and sometime favourite of Queen Isabella; passing subsequently under the direct control of the Crown. Eventually bluff King Hal presented the estate in his own freehanded way to our old acquaintance, Sir Rhys ap Thomas; and so when John Leland, the famous antiquary, travelled into South Wales upon his 'Laborious Journey, and Searche for England's Antiquities,' he duly described Narberth Castle as a 'praty pile of old Sir Rees.'

To the south of the town lies a broken, hilly district called Narberth Forest; whence were procured, in bygone days, large quantities of oak and other timber, for building the famous 'wooden walls' of the British navy. In olden times, this locality formed a favourite hunting-ground of the Knights of St. John of Jerusalem, whose custom it was to ride out from their headquarters at Slebech, and chase the wild deer that frequented its woodland glades.

The village of Templeton, (which doubtless derives its name from that martial fraternity), is now a mere rambling, skeleton of a place, with a few dwelling-houses of the better sort amongst the cottages that flank the highway. Once upon a time, it is said, Templeton could boast its village-cross and ancient wayside chapel; but of these not a solitary vestige has survived to give colour to the story.

We now approach the eastern confines of the County, and thus enter upon the beginning of the end of our Pembrokeshire peregrinations. From Templeton we set our faces towards the hamlet of Eglwys-fair-glan-Tâf, better known, probably, to the *Saesneg* traveller as Whitland railway junction.

Laying our course adown the vale of the pretty Afon Marlas, we traverse the long village street of Lampeter Velfrey; and so, keeping rail and river upon our left flank, we presently strike the course of the

infant Tâf near the old disused tollgate at Pen-y-bont. At the little
bridge that connects our County with its big neighbour of Carmarthen,
we call a halt to lounge beside the low parapet, and transfer to the
sketch-book an impression of St. Mary's Church, with the time-worn

EGLWYSFAIR GLAN TAF.

stonework of the old arches and cutwaters spanning the trout stream in
the foreground.

* * * * * *

Here, then, we bid farewell to quaint old Pembrokeshire, and
conclude our sketching rambles amidst its secluded byways.

Not many localities, we take it, can boast, within so comparatively
limited a compass, such varied attractions for the lover of old-world
associations and time-worn architecture; attractions, withal, that to

some minds are enhanced by a sense of remoteness and isolation from the ceaseless *Sturm und Drang* of modern city life.

Although far from exhausting the scope of such a many-sided subject, we venture to hope that these pages may enable our readers to participate in the unalloyed pleasure and interest we have ourselves derived, from these pen-and-pencil peregrinations amidst the Nooks and Corners of Pembrokeshire.

REDBERTH FONT.

INDEX.

29

Elliot Stock, 62, Paternoster Row, London.

LIST OF SUBSCRIBERS' NAMES.

Copies.

Allen, Very Rev. Dean, St. Davids ... 1
Arnett, J. E., Tenby 3
Baker, Rev. S. O., Somerset 1
Ballinger, J., Cardiff 1
Bellamy, C. H., Heaton Chapel ... 1
Beloe, E. M., King's Lynn 1
Berensberg, Count Victor de, Haver-
fordwest 1
Bethell, W., Malton 1
and one large.
Blanc, H. S., Edinburgh 1
Bowen, J. B., Llwyngwair, Crymmych 1
Bowen, Rev. D., Pembroke 1
Bridgman, Rev. Canon, Wigan ... 1
Brigstocke, Ll., Haverfordwest ... 12
Bromley, Rev. W., Manorbere Vicar-
age 1
Bumpus, J. and E., Limited, Holborn 1
Bute, Lord, Cardiff Castle 1
Carroway, J., Blackheath 1
Chance, R. L., Edgbaston 2
Cherwood-Aiken, J. C., Stoke Bishop 1
Codner, D. J. D., Pembrokeshire ... 1
Daltry, Rev. T. W., Newcastle ... 1
Davies, D. J., Knightsbridge... ... 1
Davies, G., Pembroke 1
Davies, Rev. G., St. Brides, Pembroke 1
Davies, Rev. W., Morlais, Fishguard 1
Davies-Burlton, T., Leominster ... 1
Davis, Mrs. Warren, Milford Haven ... 1
Dixon, W. H., 1, Arthur Road, Edg-
baston 1
Dodd, Mead, and Co., New York ... 3
and one large.
Downing, Wm., Birmingham... ... 1
Duncan, John, F.J.I., J.P., Cardiff ... 1
Elkington, G., Edgbaston 1
Evans, T. W., Fellowes Road, London 1
Feeney, John, Birmingham 1
Field, H. H., Beds 1
Gilpin, Captain N., Hove 1
Gray, Henry, Leicester Square ... 12
Greenish, R., Manorbere 1
Gwyther, F., Haverfordwest 1
Hanbury, Rev. T., Market Harborough 1
Hand, T. W., Oldham... 1

Copies.

Harries, Cecilia J., London 1
Hartwright, H., Tarporley 1
Haslam, W. F., Edgbaston 1
Haslewood, Rev. F. G., Canterbury... 1
Haynes, G. B., Brynhir, near Swan-
sea 1
Haynes, H., Harrow, Middlesex ... 1
Henman, William, F.R.I.B.A., Bir-
mingham 2
Hill, T. Rowley, Worcester 1
Hilbers, the Ven. Archdeacon, G. C.,
Haverfordwest 1
Hooke, Rev. D. Burford, High Barnet 1
Horncastle, H., Woking 1
Howell, George Owen, Plumstead ... 1
Idris, T. B. W., Camden Town ... 1
Jakeman and Carver, Hereford ... 1
John, E., Middlesborough 1
Jolly, F., Bath 1
Jones, M. T., Wrexham 1
Layton, C. Miller, Folkestone ... 1
Lester, E., Rochester 1
Lewis, Rev. David, St. Davids ... 1
Lillington, Mrs. E., Penzance ... 1
Lingard-Monk, R. B. M., Wilmslow... 1
Llewellyn, R. W., Briton Ferry ... 1
Lloyd, E. O. V., Corwen 2
Lloyd, H. Meuric, South Wales ... 1
Lloyd-Philips, F. L., Pembrokeshire 1
Maillard, Mrs., Pembroke 1
Marrs, Kingsmill, Saxonville, U.S.A.... 1
Marychurch, Wm., Cardiff 1
Mathias, H., Haverfordwest 1
Mayler, J. E., Wexford 1
Meynell, Edgar J., Durham 1
Middlemass, Major J. C., Monkton... 1
Morgan, Rev. C., Pembroke 1
Morgan, Lieut.-Col. W. L., Swansea 1
Morrison, Dr., Portclew, Pembroke 1
Nevin, J., Mirfield 1
Nield, W., Bristol 1
Oldham Central Free Library ... 1
Owen, Honourable Mrs., Treffgarn ... 1
Owen, Rev. Elias, M.A., F.S.A., Os-
westry 1
Parker, F. Rowley, Harrow Weald 1

	Copies.
Parkinson, Captain F. R., President, Garrison Library, Pembroke Dock	1
Pashley, R., Rotherham	1
Pears, Andrew, Isleworth	1
Penney, J. W., Pembroke	1
Perrott, E., West Brighton	1
Phelps, Rev. C. M., Haverfordwest ...	1
Phillips, Rev. J., Haverfordwest ...	1
Philipps, Sir Charles E. G., Bart., Lord Lieutenant, Haverfordwest... ...	1
Pierce, Ellis, Dolyddelen	1
Pollen, G. A. J., Seaton Carew ...	1
Powell, Mrs., Hereford	1
Price, Rees, Glasgow	1
Prickett, T. A., Tottenham Court Road, W.	1
Protheroe, E. S., Dolwilym	1
Randall, J., Sheffield	1
Reece, Mrs., Carpenter Road, Edgbaston	1
Rees, Griffith, Birkenhead	1
Rees, Howell, J.P., South Wales ...	1
Rees, J. Rogers, Penarth	1
Richards, D., Cardiff	1
Richards, D. M., Aberdare	1
Roberts, O. M., Portmadoc	1
Roberton, J. D., Glasgow	1
Rock, T. Dennis, South Wales ...	1
Roughsedge, Miss, Birkenhead ...	1
Rowntree, Wm., Scarborough ...	1
Samson, Louis, Haverfordwest ...	1
Sandys, Lt.-Col. T. Myles, M.P., Ulverston	1
and one large.	
Seward, E., Cardiff	1
Skrine, H. D., Bath	1
Small, Evan W., Newport	1
Society of Antiquaries...	1

	Copies.
Sparrow, A., Shrewsbury	1
Spurrell, W., and Son, Carmarthen ...	4
St. Davids, The Right Rev. the Lord Bishop of	1
Stewart, J., Llandyssil	1
Stone, Rev. D., Wallingford	1
Studholme, Paul, Parsonstown ...	1
Sturge, R. L., Bristol	1
Swansea, The Right Rev. the Lord Bishop of	1
Swinburne, Mrs. W. A., Dulais Hay...	1
Thomas, J., J.P., Haverfordwest ...	1
Thomas, T. Lynn, Cardiff	1
Thomas, Rev. F. O., Narberth ...	1
Thomas, Rev. W. Meyler, Milford Haven...	1
Thomason, Yeoville, F.R.I.B.A., Kensington	1
Timmins, F. H., Westfield Road, Edgbaston	1
Timmins, Miss, Edgbaston	1
Tredegar, Lord, Tredegar Park ...	1
Trevaldwyn, Rev. B. W. J., Looe ...	1
Treweeks, R. H.	3
and one large.	
Troutbeck, Miss, Congleton	1
Turbervill, Colonel J. P., Bridgend ...	1
Turner, W. H., Maidstone	1
Walker, W., Finsbury Park	1
Walters, Rev. T., Maenclochog ...	1
Warburton, S., Balham	1
Wharton, Rev. G., Abingdon... ...	1
Williams, G., Finsbury Pavement ...	1
Williams, J., Brook Street, W. ...	1
Williams, Wm., Aberystwyth... ...	2
Williamson, G. C., Guildford... ...	1
Wills, W. Leonard, Worcestershire ...	1
Wright, A. J., Milford Haven... ...	1

LARGE PAPER.

	Copies.
Bethell, W., Malton	1
and one small.	
Brigstocke, Ll., Haverfordwest ...	1
Brimmer, Mrs. Martin, Boston, U.S.A.	1
Dodd, Mead, and Co., New York ...	1
Gray, H., London	3
Ford, J. W., Enfield Old Park ...	1
Jones, J., 19, Cheapside, E.C. ...	1
Kensington, Lady, Pembrokeshire ...	1

	Copies.
Lambton, Lt.-Col. F. W., Pembroke...	1
Owen, Henry, 44, Oxford Terrace, W.	1
Sandys, Lt.-Col. T. Myles, M.P., Ulverston	1
and one small.	
Saunders, E. A., Pembroke Dock ...	1
Smith, R. V. Vassar, Cheltenham ...	1
Treweeks, R. H.	1
and three small.	